WALKING INTO WALLS

WALKING INTO WALLS

5 Blind Spots That Block
God's Work in You

STEPHEN ARTERBURN

WORTHY
PUBLISHING

Published by Worthy Publishing, a division of Worthy Media, Inc., 134 Franklin Road, Suite 200, Brentwood, Tennessee 37027.

HELPING PEOPLE EXPERIENCE THE HEART OF GOD

eBook available at www.worthypublishing.com

Audio distributed through Oasis Audio; visit www.oasisaudio.com

Library of Congress Control Number: 2011931409

For foreign and subsidiary rights, contact Riggins International Rights Services, Inc.; www.rigginsrights.com

ISBN: 978-1-936034-50-5 (hardcover with dustjacket)

Cover Design: Faceout Studio, Charles Brock
Interior Design and Typesetting: Inside Out Design & Typesetting

Printed in the United States of America
. 11 12 13 14 15 QGFF 8 7 6 5 4 3 2 1

To Daryn,
who has been knocking down walls
that too many people are
walking into.

Too many people live needlessly in defeat, immobilized by their own mistakes or the mistakes of others. They repeatedly walk into emotional walls that block the work God wants to do in them. It doesn't have to be this way! No matter how broken or hurt, every person can discover the way to healing, hope, and a new way of living.

CONTENTS

Acknowledgments

A huge thanks to Byron Williamson and Rob Birkhead, who made this—my favorite book—possible.

And to Tom Williams, who did a masterful job of editing and restructuring this book; you're the best.

LEARNING TO SEE OUR WALLS

A friend told me the story of a bird that wandered down a chimney and into a family residence one night. Morning came and the family discovered the terrified creature. Trapped by walls and apparently threatened by monsters suddenly appearing in the room, the panicked bird flew toward the morning sunlight streaming through the big picture window. But it crashed into the wall of glass and fell back into the room. The family tried to catch the bird and release it harmlessly through the door, but each time it would flee in panic and fly again toward the sunrise, only to hit the same wall of glass. It happened again and again because the poor creature simply could not see the barrier that blocked it from reaching what looked like glorious freedom.

WALLS OF OUR OWN

The first reaction to this story is to think that bird should have learned a lesson the first time it hit the glass. Why would it keep flying into the same barrier again and again? But, quite frankly, many of us often walk into walls, back off, collect ourselves, and then proceed to walk right back into them again. These are walls of guilt and shame, anger and bitterness, worry and regret, and fear and anxiety.

I have developed relationships in business, ministry, and my personal life that felt like prison walls. Some of those relational prisons were optional, but I chose to live with them. In my personal life, sometimes others chose to end their relationships with me, leaving me walled off inside my pitiful little cell of shame, regret, and loneliness.

I could have changed, but I kept myself locked up with beliefs that barred me from doing so. Ever said any of these things to yourself?

- "This is not my fault."
- "My parents just didn't get it."
- "Nobody can help me but me."
- "I know how to deal with this on my own."
- "I am not the one with the problem here."
- "How could this person hurt me, knowing what a victim of others I have been?"
- "You have to be crazy to see a counselor."

- "Anyone would feel this way if he or she knew what I have been through."

- "When the person who hurt me makes a move toward resolution, I am prepared to respond, but not until then."

- "I'm so guilty that God can never forgive me, so I'm now on my own."

I had a lot of other erroneous beliefs rolling around in my head that became barrier walls, keeping me from a life of freedom, purpose, and meaning. Yet I kept these beliefs in front of me, encountering them again and again. Each encounter became more painful than the pain that would have been involved in tearing down those walls and moving into freedom. While in college I thought I had made so much progress with myself that I should make a career out of helping others. The real truth was, I had no idea how little progress I had made, how far I had to go, and how much more pain I would have to endure.

POTTY TRAINING

In 1977 I began my studies in counseling at a seminary in Fort Worth, Texas. For the first time I looked forward to every day of school. Very quickly I was involved in doctoral courses and providing counseling under the supervision of doctoral students. I loved it and believed, as I still do, that I had found my purpose: to help people with emotional and mental problems.

As I progressed I wanted to gain experience with those struggling with the worst of psychiatric diagnoses. The only job I could find was as an attendant on a psychiatric ward, and I took it with great excitement and dedication. My job description was to help in any way needed. That meant counseling a newly admitted patient or cleaning toilets. In my ascent from custodian to chief therapist, I saw nearly every kind of emotional and mental damage. Much of it was inflicted by cruel and heartless perpetrators who ripped normalcy out of patients' lives and left them with scarred souls.

At first I could not understand the depths of evil committed against the innocent. One man's moment of sexual gratification often destroyed the healthy and happy life of another. I don't have research figures, but I would guess that one moment of illicit sexual gratification produces ten thousand moments of pain and suffering during the lifetime of a victim.

It wasn't just men who wreaked havoc on the lives of the young. Mothers did it too. Some smothered, even trapped their young to always be there for them throughout their entire lives. Never free to become independent adults, these tethered people collapsed into psychiatric care, not understanding why life was so unmanageable or their minds so filled with conflict. Unexpressed rage and ungrieved loss piled on top of confusion and disappointment.

THE MYSTERY OF MISERY

Every patient I counseled was a mystery. Was his problem perpetrated upon him, or was he born with a genetic predisposition to experience the downside of life? Had she had a harder life than others, or had she simply been less equipped to deal with life's realities? The mysteries of the causes of emotional and mental dysfunction were just the beginning. Beyond those was the mystery of how some made their way out of the morass of terrible despair into fully functional lives.

What struck me most about these extreme cases was this: if these patients who had experienced the worst could overcome what troubled them, there was good reason for hope for those who were not in such bad shape. Relationships could be healed, inner conflict and struggle could be resolved, and addicts could recover.

So the question was, why did some patients lose themselves after great loss, while others *found* themselves and moved past their walls into new lives? I learned that the better outcome is often due to how a person sees life in light of his past and current relationships, as well as how others see him. Millions of people are still hurting over something that may have happened years ago. It has become a wall they cannot get past. Rather than resolve the pain and move on, such broken people continue to bump against that wall, living as if that painful past were a present reality. They judge themselves and others based on an event that could have been resolved long ago. Their wall becomes a past that cannot be changed, and so they will not move on until those who hurt them remove the wall by making a change. That change rarely occurs, leaving the wall intact and the emotions and faith of the injured person impaired. Thus wounded and confined, the injured person goes on facing life in a negative, self-defeating way.

Introduction

Deal with the Wall or Remain in Misery

Too many people live needlessly in defeat, immobilized by their own mistakes or the mistakes of others. They repeatedly walk into emotional walls that block the work God wants to do in them. It does not have to be this way! No matter how broken or hurt, every person can discover the way to healing, hope, and a new way of living. Walls of pain erected by past traumas need not be the obstacles they so often become. Getting past these walls means seeing them for what they are, finding the lies they present and the truths they hide, or finding the door in the wall that will allow us to move on. The important thing to remember is this: no matter how big or impassable your wall seems to be, there is always a way to get past it. Always. There is a way around it, through it, over it, or there is a way to take the wall down. Walking into walls may be inevitable, but staying stuck behind them is not. You can get past your wall, and that is what this little book will show you how to do.

Jacob Witting's Wall

The movie *Winter's End* of the Sarah, Plain and Tall series illustrates what it means to have a wall built on past hurt. It tells the story of Jacob Witting (Christopher Walken), a Midwestern farmer, and his wife, Sarah (Glenn Close). It is set during World War I, and the family enjoys a hard but good life with three children in a small, rural community.

Early in the story Jacob's father, John Witting (Jack Palance), suddenly shows up. He is aged and ill and apparently a drifter with no means of support. He had abandoned his wife and son when the boy was in grade school, and he has never contacted the family since. Jacob actually thought the man was dead.

Jacob Witting deeply resents his father for the abandonment, and he wants the man out of his house. Sarah, however, talks Jacob into allowing his father to stay until he is at least well enough to travel.

When Jacob is injured in an angry confrontation with his father, the older man must stay on to help with the farm. During this time the family begins to accept him—that is, everyone but Jacob, whose bitterness is a wall that he cannot get past.

But Sarah finally talks Jacob into at least hearing his father's side of the story. There may be more to it than Jacob knows. Jacob relents and has the talk. He learns that the circumstances of his father's leaving were not at all what he had assumed. His mother, raised in a prosperous eastern family, had deeply resented the hard farm life marriage had imposed on her. Her resentment was so deep that John Witting had come to believe that the only way she could be happy was for him to get out of her life. So he left. He wrote letters to his son, but his bitter wife never passed them on to the boy. John explains that, looking back, he realized that leaving was the wrong thing to do.

With his father's explanation and confession, Jacob's wall crumbles, and he accepts his father fully into the family.

THE NEED FOR NEW LIGHT

You may never understand relationship barriers in the present until you see your past in a whole new light. Often the hurt we feel in the wake of a traumatic event becomes the lens through which we view ourselves and those involved in the incident. That lens of pain can distort the truth or some part of the truth and leave us facing a wall of bitterness or rejection or a damaged self-image that we cannot get past. If you have lost your freedom and hope because you are trapped behind walls of old patterns of thinking, you can begin to live a new life. You can view your past—and your present—with pain-free clarity rather than through the lens of your heartache and hurt. If you have never fully achieved all you thought you could or wanted, you can find a new way to break through the wall that holds you back and focus on your goals and your future.

FROM TRAUMA TO TRIUMPH

About twenty years ago, a young woman was jogging through Central Park in New York City when she was attacked, raped, bludgeoned, beaten, and left for dead. She was found dangerously close to death with massive skull fractures and more than half her blood lost. Her condition was so severe, and her body and brain injuries so grave, that emergency room physicians suggested to her parents that it might be best if she died.

But she did not die. She lived and began the arduous task of relearning the simplest of life skills, such as eating, walking, talking, and writing. Her recovery was remarkable because she did not allow what happened to her in the park to become a wall that blocked her life. While some would have personalized the vicious attack, this woman came to see it as a random act of violence. While some might have wanted an apology or vengeance, she required nothing from the attackers. While some would have felt like a victim, she began to see herself as a victorious survivor. She refused to let a past she could not change become a wall that barred her future. She resolved the horrific emotions that resulted from her tragedy and then went on to refocus her life entirely.

This heroic woman now speaks regularly to survivors of trauma, rape, and acts of violence. She is an inspiration to anyone fortunate enough to hear her speak.

This book is about the process of getting past barriers created by guilt, fear, and anger. It's about gaining new information and insight into traumatic events, both past and present, and moving toward resetting your perspective in order to free yourself to move past the barriers they have created. The intent is to help you refocus, move on past the wall, and live with new purpose and meaning.

Seeing reality from a new perspective liberates you to live with less pain and conflict, full of purpose and meaning, and free from a past that cannot be changed. If you are willing to step back, take a second look, and do some work, this could be the beginning of a whole new life for you. If you are ready, let's get to work on moving past the walls you keep walking into. It could make all the difference in your life.

The walls that hold us back are often constructions built in our own minds from incomplete or misunderstood pieces of reality and combined half-truths woven together in a way that builds a false perception of the truth. In that sense, what often stops us are barriers that aren't really there.

chapter one

PHANTOM WALLS THAT STOP US

Sometimes when I want to just put my mind in neutral and be entertained, I will flip the TV remote to *America's Funniest Home Videos*. One of the funniest and most telling video clips involves a house cat at the back door of a home. The door is a common type—an aluminum frame designed to encase a single, solid panel of glass. In the clip the cat is at the door meowing to get out. What the cat does not realize is that there is no glass in the door frame. It had apparently been broken out. The man of the house comes and tries to urge the cat on through the empty space, but the cat will not go. The man even steps through the open frame to show the cat it can be done, but the cat still refuses to budge. It is not until the man opens the door and allows the cat to scurry around the frame that it goes out to freedom.

Much of the time the walls that hold us back are no more real than the absent glass in that door frame. I don't mean that they are not really barriers; I mean they are often constructions built in our own minds from incomplete or misunderstood pieces of reality and combined half-truths woven together in such a way that builds a false perception of the truth. In that sense, what often stops us are barriers that are not really there. They are fabricated entirely, or at least mostly, in our own minds.

We are all guilty of this. We take fragments of reality and a few half-truths and build concepts that are not exactly accurate. Because of these lies that circulate in our heads, we build barriers of anger and resentment about things others have done, or guilt about things that were not our fault. We may view some of our strengths as weaknesses and define ourselves inaccurately, exaggerating all that is wrong and crowding out all that is good and strong and capable.

Maybe you have built a phantom wall by making someone else responsible for something that is clearly your own doing. You may be married to a fairly normal person with fairly normal problems, but you manage to blame your spouse for all your difficulties. You play the role of victim, blaming others for all that's wrong in your life, and the blame becomes a wall in your mind that holds you back just as effectively as if it were real. But it is *not* real. Those you frame to take the rap for your *stuff* may actually be guilty of many things, but they are not responsible for all the things that have gone wrong in your life. They are especially not responsible for the wall you have built in your mind in response to their actions.

THE IMPORTANCE OF NEW PERSPECTIVE

The new perspective we need in getting past our walls is more than just seeing the upside of the dark and traumatic experiences in life. It is not a matter of merely seeing the glass as half full. It is looking at life from a broader perspective than just one painful event. It is looking deeper into all the facts surrounding the past rather than personalizing the hurt. We often carry destructive thoughts around with us that may not exactly fit the real facts. We know the story of what happened, but it may not be a completely accurate story. In our pain, resentment, or anger, we may have assumed things that were not true.

Adoption can be an example of inaccurate perception. It often leads to feelings of rejection. Adopted children can assume there must be something wrong with them, or their birth mother would not have given them up. Yes, giving up a child for adoption does involve some form of rejection, but it is rarely as evil or as personal as many adopted kids think. If you were given up for adoption, your mother did not reject you, the person you are now. And her motives for giving you up were likely related to wanting something better for your life than she thought she could give. Almost all who give up their children do so with a tremendous amount of reluctance and grief.

Adopted children need not let their birth mothers' choices become walls. They can come to see that they were not personally rejected. Their parents rejected only the concept of a child and all that a child demands and needs. It was *not* personal. It could not have been personal because she had no way of knowing you as the person you are now. It was a decision made by a parent struggling to survive, feeling inadequate to raise a child, and wanting the best for her child. First, your mother made a decision for you to live. She did not abort you. She chose life for you. Then she chose a better life for you than she could provide. Seeing this truth can bring down the wall of rejection.

Jesus was intent on getting people to see the truth. That is why he so often challenged the way they looked at life and each other. He would sometimes say, "You have heard it said . . ." and then quote some established belief. Then he would counter that common wisdom with, "But I say . . ." and proceed to astound listeners with an amazing new perspective on the old way of thinking.

Jesus' philosophy could be summarized this way: Life is not all about you, it is not all about your things, and it is not even all about this world. It is not all about feeling good or getting what you want. It is not about what you think you need right now. It is about another world beyond Earth and an inner world of the heart without conflict or pretense. Jesus made a difference two thousand years ago because he challenged people to see things from a true perspective. The old way created barriers because it was not based on reality. Living with and in the truth sets us free. It is another way of saying that understanding reality removes walls.

HISTORY REPEATED

Getting past a wall could mean learning more about the history of the person who rejected or abused you and discovering the origins of the rejection or abuse. At a workshop I conducted in Southern California, I worked with a young man whose life was blocked by a wall of anger at his mother. When he was an infant, his mother left him on a neighbor's front porch and abandoned him. He was in a rage now because, after all these years, she wanted back into his life.

At my suggestion he was able to work through the incident and see it through a clearer lens. I instructed him to call his mother and ask about her childhood. Maybe it would reveal her reasons for making the decision to leave him. The next day he came back in tears. His mother had told him of how her mother had done the same thing to her, but she never came back. Now she was trying to turn a page and be something better than her own mother had been.

Seeing the whole truth behind the traumatic event removed the wall for this man. It freed him from this barrier from the past that blocked his present. It allowed him to resolve his negative emotions, refocus his life, and develop a deep bond with his mother.

Many parents and children are estranged from each other, not realizing that they actually share a bond of neglect, a common experience of pain, and a mutual battle to move beyond walls of resentment and bitterness.

When an abandoned or abused person comes up for air from a life of bitterness, anger, and resentment, he can come to see that he did not have the whole story. The heartless person who inflicted the hurt may have found a heart, and the pain the victim feels may be that person's biggest regret.

BUT MY ABUSE WAS REAL

At this point you may be thinking, *This book is not for me because I really am being abused,* or *This is not for me because the horror of my childhood is not a phantom wall. It is not something I just made up; it happened.* If those are your thoughts, or anything close, I hope you will read on, because I am very aware of real abuse in the past and living with impossible people in the present. I do not discount your pain for one second. Life for many is a living hell.

But I would not be writing this if I did not believe the worst situations can be helped. Even if you were living in the worst possible abusive situation or the most neglectful and disconnected relationship, you may have built a wall that keeps you stuck in a dark place where you don't have to stay. Children are not responsible for the abuse that robs them of their childhood, but as adults they are responsible for their reactions to that early life—reactions that could rob them of a meaningful adulthood. Once you take responsibility, you will find new hope and insight as you get your life unstuck and move past your wall.

We become the kings of stubborn resistance in our own little worlds. We get into ruts that lead us down paths that cause nothing but pain and end with our hitting a wall. Yet we will do everything but try something different.

chapter two

THE WALL OF STUBBORN RESISTANCE

Twice a year I serve as host and speaker of a nationwide intensive workshop on weight loss called Lose It for Life. Each time, I am astonished at the people who have journeyed from all over the country to come. Some have had to endure the embarrassment of purchasing two airline seats just to accommodate their bulk. Many come in wheelchairs, because their weight prevents them from walking easily, if at all. Oxygen tubes run from tanks to their noses, because they are no longer able to breathe well on their own.

When I see these people, I think of the line from the movie *The Sixth Sense* when the little boy said, "I see dead people." It truly looks as if the life has gone out of these wonderful people. You would think that in their plight they would all be highly motivated to hear new things and try new ways of losing weight and keeping it off. But that is not necessarily so.

On the first night during the first session, I stand before them and say, "All of you in this room have something in common, and it is not just a struggle with your weight. Every person here struggles with what I call 'stubborn resistance.' In fact some of you have built your whole identity around resisting anything that anyone else suggests. If someone says 'white,' you will automatically respond with 'black.' If someone says, 'Go to the right,' you will veer to the left. You have a hard time going along with what others think.

"For some of you the stubborn resistance is so strong you actually came here to prove you could *not* be helped. You may not realize it, but you came here to solidify your belief that you know everything there is to know about weight loss, and no one knows you and your needs well enough to help you. But if you don't give up your stubborn resistance, you will leave here not having heard, not having shared, and not having risked taking the step that could make your life completely different from what it is now."

Don't misunderstand me. It was not stubborn resistance that made these people overweight. That was a combination of the foods they ate, the exercise they chose, the attitudes they carried, and the genes they inherited. But it is stubborn resistance that keeps them stuck in their overweight condition. Stubborn resistance can prevent them from seeing their blind spot and thus feeds the belief that there is no hope for getting past the wall that prevents them from experiencing a new life.

Fortunately, because we talk about this right up front, many attendees are open-minded enough to be alert to the possibility of a blind spot and to accept the implication that their continued inability to move past the walls of their weight might be partly their own doing. With that kind of openness, many who have held on to their stubborn resistance since childhood are able to see it and find a new path filled with hope and potential. They not only lose weight and reconstruct their external realities, but they also address the negative internal constructs that have fed their cravings for more food than they need.

The "It"

As long as these people believe the walls they can't get past are their weight, they still have blind spots, and they will keep walking into the real walls they cannot see. A deeper reality is the real problem, and I call that reality the "it." Most people come believing the "it" is their need to lose weight. But during the course of the weekend, they come to realize "it" means much more than weight. As long as weight is the only issue they attend to, the factors causing the weight problem will go unaddressed. Those who do well in the workshop discover that the "it" they need to address is the guilt and shame they have been carrying around since experiencing some extraordinarily painful event in their past. If they don't lose that "it," any attempt to lose weight will be temporary and will only add to their frustrations as they continue to feed the "it," and the weight comes back, usually worse than ever before.

Once people go after the "it" behind the weight problem, they break through their stubborn resistance and are on their way to making real progress—not just in losing the weight on their bodies, but losing the weight on their souls. That in turn leads to keeping the weight off for good.

RESISTING THE LOSS OF OUR STUBBORN RESISTANCE

If you are not overweight, you might look at one of these strugglers and say, "How can a person one hundred pounds overweight stubbornly resist the help that could free her from her weight?" But if you are like me, while my body does not show an obvious problem with weight, inside my soul—and inside yours—there are problems just as big that need attention. It's that old problem of twenty-twenty vision when we look into the lives of others and blindness when we look at ourselves.

Now, be honest: When you started reading this chapter about stubborn resistance, did you immediately start thinking about people you know who exhibit that trait? It's so easy to point at someone else, because that keeps the attention off of me. It's easy to point the finger at those who have *obvious* problems; it's tougher to examine my own life to see if I am displaying some other form of this paralyzing stubborn resistance. But if I want to get past my walls, I must stop the finger pointing and consider whether I might harbor the same trait. As Pogo the possum used to say in the old comic strip, "We have met the enemy, and he is us."

When you are stuck in stubborn resistance, you may hear words that would help you move past your walls but refuse to attend to them. You defend and rationalize your behaviors and attitudes. You project your problem onto someone else, blaming others or circumstances for the way you are. You become reactive to those who challenge you, because you will do anything you can to protect the wall you have created to avoid the pain of self-examination. You are not open to attempting a different way of thinking or living because you are afraid of losing the comfort of having that wall of dysfunction to hide behind.

The Bible confronts us directly about stubborn resistance in Acts 7:51: "You stubborn people! You are heathen at heart and deaf to the truth. Must you forever resist the Holy Spirit? That's what your ancestors did, and so do you!" (NLT). If you will let him, God can use the words of this book, the words of Scripture, the words of others, impressions on your heart, and your own gut feelings to help you move beyond the wall of your stubborn resistance.

THE KING OF STUBBORN RESISTANCE

Many people hang on to stubborn resistance, just as Pharaoh did in the days of Moses. Moses went to Pharaoh and asked to lead the Israelites out of Egypt. Pharaoh resisted with entrenched stubbornness. So God sent plagues on Pharaoh's nation to turn his thinking around. Now, if I had been Pharaoh, I might also have resisted Moses' request to let my slaves just walk out of my country. But after the gnats, it would not have been a problem at all. If not the gnats, the flies surely would have turned my heart. One fly is enough for me. I know where those dirty, hairy little legs have been. But massive swarms of gnats and flies were not enough to break through Pharaoh's stubborn resistance. Nor were painful, infectious boils that broke out all over him and the bodies of his people. He remained stubborn through plague after plague, each one worse than the one before, until Egypt was utterly devastated. But still he stubbornly resisted, finally to his own undoing.

We do the same thing. We become the kings of stubborn resistance in our own little worlds. We get into ruts that lead us down paths that cause nothing but pain and end with our hitting walls. Yet we will do everything but try something different. We develop habits and hang-ups we will not even think of releasing. We hurt ourselves and those around us, allowing boils to fester in almost every area of life. The boils grow and become infected; yet we still cling to our right to do what we please. Or we demand that others cater to the pain we are in, refusing to budge past our self-created walls of stubborn resistance.

How we can endure so much loss and pain and yet refuse to seek help remains a mystery. But it happens. Rather than looking for ways past the walls, we hang on to our right to remain the same, our right to live our lives as we choose, no matter how painful those lives might become.

OUR STUBBORNLY RESISTANT HERITAGE

I guess I have been pretty hard on you so far, insisting on the probability that somewhere in your life you likely exhibit some form of stubborn resistance. But now I want to give you a little break. Most of us don't come by these traits solely on our own.

Often we learn them from parents or grandparents who mastered the art.

I came from an extremely stubborn family that did not want to be told there was a better way. My grandfather was the most hardheaded man I have ever known. I admired his unwavering confidence, but it often got in the way of anything in which he was involved. And I have found myself living in his hand-me-down genes many times.

My grandfather lived on a lake in a house he had built with his five sons. They first built it as a small cabin with a huge porch that could sleep about twenty people. The family outgrew the little cabin, so they added on.

The expanded structure turned out to be a nice place, more than doubling the size of the original cabin. But it had one major flaw. My grandfather had not calculated into the ceiling height the fact that the new addition had a foundation about twelve inches higher than that of the original cabin. So the ceiling in the new area was a foot lower than it was supposed to be. I felt as if I needed to hunch over when I was in the big room. If I was not looking, I could walk right into the ceiling fan and permanently injure myself. And it was all because of my stubborn grandfather. His sons told him from the beginning what was wrong with the plans, but he would not listen because he was sure he was always right.

Those raised in such a family can come to believe that is how people normally relate. Each person takes a position and defends it. Anyone suggesting a new or different way does not understand that there is a tradition to uphold or a pattern to follow. So generation after generation, the family holds on to its sick ground, no one changing and everyone living behind walls (or under low ceilings), disconnected from truly intimate relationships.

The other break I can give is to those who grew up in families so sick that the only way they could survive was to stake out their individual territories and hold on. They had a hard enough time just getting from one moment to the next, and stubborn resistance became a defense that helped them live to see another day.

So don't beat yourself up over how your stubborn resistance has hurt you. Feel good about the fact that now you see it as a wall, because that new clarity enables you to do something about it. You no longer need to be among those who continue to walk into walls because they hold on to old destructive patterns of stubbornness alongside resistence.

Willingness: The Key to Overcoming Stubborn Resistance

If you realize you have a tendency toward stubborn resistance, be grateful, because it is not easy for people to see their need to change in this area. More commonly, stubbornly resistant people view themselves as extremely confident. Even if you get beyond that confident rationalization and see the need to change, stubborn resistance by its very nature is stubbornly resistant to change. So don't expect to overcome it in a moment or a day. It will take time and work.

The First Step: Open-Mindedness

While the key to overcoming stubborn resistance is willingness, we are seldom willing to change unless we first see the need. We will never see the need to become willing to change unless we first pry our minds open and look at situations objectively. Looking at situations objectively is perhaps the most difficult attitude for any stubbornly resistant person to adopt. But opening our minds to the possibility of other points of view is the only way to remove the walls that hold us back. We must learn to see our lives in a whole new light, from a more objective viewpoint than just our own opinions of how things should be.

If you question whether you are stubbornly resistant, ask yourself these self-evaluation questions, do your best to open your mind to the truth, and answer honestly:

- How frequently do I admit I was wrong?

- How frequently do I ask for forgiveness?

- How frequently do I ask people for their opinions?

- Do I ever admit that I have been approaching problems in unhealthy ways?

- Am I willing to admit that I might need help to move beyond the walls in my life?

- Have I ever said, "You knew I was this way when you married me"?

- Do people tell me, or do I feel, that I have a strong need always to be right?

- Do I stop listening to people who try to get me to see things in different ways?

- Am I a "my way or the highway" kind of person?

These questions can clue you in to your level of open-mindedness. Open-mindedness is characterized by the ability to see things from another person's perspective, or at least to be interested enough to acknowledge that there are other points of view to be considered. Open-minded people realize not only that they are not always right but also that they need to make things right when they are wrong. Open-minded people are able to be quiet for a while and listen to someone else who might have something valuable to contribute. Open-minded people become willing to consider recovery or counseling, because they know there is a world of vital and helpful information available that they could never find on their own.

MOVING ON TO WILLINGNESS

Open-mindedness is a valuable assessment tool, but it is worthless unless it is followed up with a willingness to act. Open-mindedness is the prerequisite; willingness is the actual key to overcoming stubborn resistance. Some people have all sorts of plans they never accomplish and dreams they never experience. Over and over they sigh and moan about how great things would have been had they been able to pull off what they intended. They *intended* to make the birthday really special. They *wanted* to get to that meeting. They had *plans* to call that counselor. But somehow they just never got it done.

A person with willingness goes beyond good intentions. There is no "try" or "want to" for the willing. The willing actually get things done. Willingness means moving beyond desire to doing whatever it takes to make things different. It is realizing that if I don't attend that meeting, I will not get feedback on my situation or problems. Therefore I am willing to take care of every obstacle that stands in the way. Willingness leads to real change.

I love the story of three men discussing their funerals. One man says, "When mourners look down at me in my coffin, I want them to say I was a good man." The second man says, "I want them to look down at my casket and say I was a good father." The third man says, "I want them to look down into my casket and say, 'He's moving! He's alive!'"

I guess we all would love to have a second chance at life. I hate to be the one to tell you, but it's not going to happen. You've got one shot at it. Live that shot with stubborn resistance doggedly entrenched, and you will live behind a wall that blocks you from all your life could be. But it doesn't have to be that way. You can get beyond any wall and into real freedom if you will do the real work of replacing that stubborn resistance with an open-minded willingness to give your life an objective look, listen to the wisdom of others, and move toward real change.

Mature adults learn that their adolescent, self-centered sense of entitlement keeps running them into walls. They learn from experience to stop doing whatever they feel entitled to do, and they start doing the things that lead to positive long-term results. When we're stuck in self-centered entitlement, we . . . remain on the paths we have chosen for ourselves, which lead to walls that block the full lives we are meant to live.

chapter three

THE WALL OF ARROGANT ENTITLEMENT

In my other life, I am a singer. Not a professional singer, but a pretty good karaoke singer. I know that confession probably diminishes respect for me in the eyes of some readers, but I sing karaoke because it really is a lot of fun. I have actually won a few competitions, always by singing Frank Sinatra songs. The winning number in my first competition was one of Frank's biggest hits: "My Way."

"My Way" is a great song with strong lyrics, a catchy melody, a huge finish, and no doubt one of the most arrogant songs ever written. In this song Frank says that he has pretty much done everything just the way he wanted to do it, and what's more, he's had so few regrets about what he's done that they're not even worth mentioning. How arrogant can you get? Perhaps the song caught on because it expresses a deep desire in the hearts of most people. Every one of us wants to live his or her life "my way."

We live in a world that encourages my-way thinking. We are bombarded with ads that tell us to "have it your way" and "you deserve a break today." Go out there and get what you deserve, no matter what it does to others. Buy this luxury product because you deserve it. You are entitled to be happy, so if you are not getting what makes you happy in your work or in your relationships, you're entitled to find it somewhere else and in some other way. After all, isn't life really all about *you* and having it *your* way?

The Bridge to Immorality

That kind of thinking causes an internal conflict, because most people know in their hearts what they should and should not do. The Bible contradicts self-oriented living by telling us not to demand our own way but to live with a strong concern for others. So when people want to tap into their feelings of self-centered, arrogant entitlement, their consciences need bridges to justify taking them from what they know is right to the places where they can indulge in what they know is not right. It's what we call *rationalization.*

Most people feel compelled to rationalize their actions when they do wrong. Otherwise, their consciences will sting them. So the person who takes home from work a box of pens or a computer program convinces himself that he is not stealing; he is really worth more than he's being paid, and he's merely evening things out by taking that to which he is entitled.

One of the saddest situations I have seen involved infidelity within the marriage of a young couple. The betrayal was on the part of the woman, who had developed a sexual addiction. She was a Christian whose previous marriage had ended in divorce. But before her divorce was final, she began to sleep around with several men who provided her with financial support as long as she was sexually involved with them. They bought her cars and helped her with bills, and in return she satisfied their sexual desires and hers as well. She felt *entitled* to the sex her divorce had deprived her of, and it also got her what she wanted.

A young man in this woman's church was not aware of her history, and he fell madly in love with her. He had also been divorced, but he was determined to save himself for his next wife. When he began dating this woman, he even resisted her attempts to have sex because he wanted to honor God with his sexual behavior.

After a year of dating, they married and went on a honeymoon where things did not go so well. She did not find the sex with her husband as exciting as with some of the men she had dated. She felt entitled to a great sex life, and rather than having the patience to allow the natural sexual adjustments of a new marriage to develop, her imagination began to wander. She began to seek attention from other men. When one responded to her enticement, she ended up having sex with him in the backseat of the car her new husband had given her. Six months later, she confessed the affair to him.

Her confession knocked the young husband for a loop. He was so deeply depressed, he wondered if he could recover. He had admired this woman and thought she was the first person who really loved him, only to discover she loved no one but herself. His heart was so broken that there were days when he could not talk. Her feelings of selfish and arrogant entitlement to sex, whether she was single or married, completely overrode all conviction of right and wrong and cavalierly plowed under the feelings and needs of her husband. Her actions left him a heap of devastated rubble. There is more to this couple's story, but I'm going to save it for later in the chapter.

This young woman did not set out to have an affair. But she was not satisfied in her marriage, and she felt entitled to be happy at all costs, no matter whom it hurt. All she cared about was having her own selfish needs met. So she felt justified in getting closer and closer to the man in the next cubicle. Soon, lust and passion shoved aside her sense of right and wrong, and she found an acceptable rationalization to create a bridge from what she knew to be right to the pleasure and happiness she told herself she was entitled to have. She enabled the betrayal by convincing herself that her action was justifiable, saying such things as:

- "I deserve this."

- "I have real needs that my husband is *not* meeting."

- "I am in a crisis, and this one thing will ease it."

- "This really isn't betrayal because I do still love my husband, and he won't ever know."

- "My husband's really disappointed me. So it's really his fault."

- "Anyone in my situation would do the same thing."

- "I'm not fully responsible because I'm an addict."

If you say these things to yourself enough, you will eventually build a bridge that enables you to cross over into arrogant entitlement. You will rationalize your action in a way that makes the wrong seem quite acceptable, given the circumstances.

This indulgence in arrogant entitlement tends to start small, but like a tiny virus, it will grow to infect every area of your life. Ultimately it will destroy your relationships and your ability to heal them. To use another metaphor, self-centered, arrogant entitlement is a bottomless pit that can never be filled. Each attempt will leave you feeling dissatisfied and always wanting more, always believing you deserve more than you have, but never quite having all you think you deserve.

If you stay on the course of arrogant entitlement, you will always be looking for the next thing or the next person to help you get what you want. You will become a taker, a self-absorbed, greedy person who uses people, takes what you can from them, and then moves on, disconnecting completely and discarding relationships like used tissue.

THE ADOLESCENT MIND-SET

Arrogant entitlement is an adolescent state of mind. It's the way we all tend to think when we hit puberty. Teenagers feel entitled to new freedoms and experiences. If parents tell a teen that a new car will not accompany his new driver's license, he is amazed at his parents' insensitivity and cruelty. If they forbid their teen to view any kind of movie she deems fit to see, she is aghast at their unreasonable strictness. Her adolescent sense of entitlement is affronted.

Of course, adolescents don't think they are acting in an immature way. They are blind to the truth because they have not gained the wisdom to see themselves objectively. As we reach adulthood, we should gain this wisdom and learn to see the truth about ourselves and change it. But for too many of us, the sense of self-centered, arrogant entitlement persists. It has been a problem with humans since Adam and Eve rejected God's rule and declared themselves king and queen of their own lives.

If you are living in self-centered entitlement and demanding to live your life "your way," you may see yourself as the center of your universe—as king or queen of your territory. If you persist in living like self-appointed royalty, others will start to see you that way as well. But this is not the good news you may think it is. To them, you will be Your Royal Highness Baby or Sir Brat the Prince. You will be the emperor with no clothes. They see right through you. You want what you want when you want it, and when you don't get it, you are angry. You are always grasping for more than you have and believing you deserve all you can get.

Naturally, self-centered people do not see themselves that way. All they want from others is what's "due" them. They have staked out their territory, and they expect everyone to honor their boundaries and their rules. In short, they are stuck in an immature way of thinking.

Mature adults learn that their adolescent, self-centered sense of entitlement keeps running them into walls. They learn from experience to stop doing whatever they feel entitled to do, and they start doing the things that lead to positive long-term results. They also broaden their viewpoint from self-absorption to include the needs of others.

When we're stuck in self-centered entitlement, we never reach that level of concern for others. We remain on the paths we have chosen for ourselves, which lead to walls that block the full life we are meant to live.

Humility: The Key to Overcoming Arrogant Entitlement

The key to overcoming arrogant entitlement is humility. Humility eliminates the self-centered arrogance that results in entitlement. It is the opposite of the me-first, my-way, give-me-what-I-deserve ways of thinking. Humility does not climb over others. It reaches out to connect with others, appreciating them for who they are, not for what they can do for you. A humble person does not use everything within himself to further his own cause, but rather he desires to use whatever strength or position he has to help others and meet their needs. As a result, the relational wall comes down, giving him access to a rich life full of valuable connections with family and friends, amassing moments of wonder where others have been helped by the efforts of a humble heart reaching out.

Humility doesn't come easy in our world. Advertising, pop psychology, and self-help gurus urge us to believe we deserve a lot of pleasure and satisfaction and to take active steps to get every bit of it. For Christians, that old capacity for rationalization often kicks in, baptizing our pursuit of self-interest with the idea that God truly does *help those who help themselves.* This phrase is often erroneously attributed to the Bible, but search from Genesis to Revelation, and you'll never find it. What the Bible does say is this: "So humble yourselves under the mighty power of God, and at the right time he will lift you up in honor" (1 Peter 5:6 NLT).

If you make this verse your guide, you will have no need for self-centeredness or feelings of entitlement. A good way to begin is to make it a habit to start each morning working on your relationship with God. Before you begin your day, ask him for help in surrendering everything to him and humbling yourself before him. Ask for the connection between you and God to grow, so you are waiting on him rather than expecting others to cater to you. This is never easy, because "his good time" is likely a whole lot slower than you want. But what a life you will have when it has the full support of the all-powerful God!

Jesus did not just tell us to be humble; he showed us how. One of the most profound examples of this occurred before the Passover meal on the night before his crucifixion. Knowing this torturous event was ahead, he could have decided he was entitled to be treated like a king and served by his loyal followers. After all, he was about to give up everything and endure unspeakable pain and suffering for the benefit of others. But instead of expecting a little consideration during his last meal, he did the most unexpected thing: he went to his knees and humbly served his disciples by performing a menial servant's task. The apostle John gives us the account:

> Jesus knew that the Father had put all things under his power,
> and that he had come from God and was returning to God;

so he got up from the meal, took off his outer clothing, and wrapped a towel around his waist. After that, he poured water into a basin and began to wash his disciples' feet, drying them with the towel that was wrapped around him. (John 13:3–5)

What an example! Jesus, the creator and sustainer of the entire universe, was entitled to everything, but he demanded nothing. He showed us that no matter who we are or what we face, we should never miss an opportunity to be humble before others. Rather than assert our rights, we should give others the right-of-way. The more self-centered and arrogantly entitled we feel, the more difficult that is. But the more humility we gain in the defeat of arrogant entitlement, the stronger we become. As the papa cow, Ben, in the movie *Barnyard* said, "A strong man stands up for himself. A stronger man stands up for others."

HUMILITY IN ACTION

Let's return to the man whose wife had an affair because she felt entitled to better sex than she thought he gave her on their honeymoon. He was a Christian and wanted to do the right thing, but he was profoundly hurt. He felt a strong urge to divorce the woman and start over with his life. He knew he needed to forgive her, and he wanted to do it, but he did not know how to overcome the hurt or the fact that she had played him for a fool. She had selfishly taken from another woman's husband what she thought she deserved, not caring that it was terribly wrong and causing her own husband to grieve as a broken man. Eventually he planned an act of humility that would help him forgive and move on rather than hold a grudge and resent her or leave her.

The idea came when he was reading the story quoted earlier about Jesus washing the feet of his disciples. He could not get out of his head the picture of Jesus on his knees before these selfish and immature men who would soon abandon, betray, and deny him in his most trying hour. He realized that if Jesus, who was God on Earth, could humble himself before these undeserving, sinful men, he certainly should be able to do it before this undeserving, sinful woman.

He invited his wife into the bathroom for a shower. He turned out the lights, and they could barely see each other's silhouettes. The atmosphere took on the aura of the sacred rather than the sexual. He moved her under the warm shower and began to shampoo her hair.

Their eyes never met as he washed her from top to bottom. When he got to her sexual parts, they both began to cry. He continued to wash her, working his way down to her feet. Slowly he washed her feet and rinsed them as he had the rest of her body. When he finished, they faced each other in the dark and hugged as they both sobbed.

The dramatic act of a man washing and cleansing his wife was symbolic of what this man wanted for her and for their marriage. This symbolic act became an invaluable image that aided their desire to move forward. It gave him a vision of where he was going—to that day when he would see her as pure and clean again. For her, it provided an image of what she wanted to feel, and it helped her deal with the shame she had brought upon herself and their marriage.

This man's act of love bathed his wife in a renewal of cleanness and forgiveness, and it freed both of them to do the work needed to hold their shaken relationship together. By anyone's standards, he was entitled to divorce her, but he fought down this self-oriented impulse and instead acted in selfless humility, showing forgiveness to her and enabling both of them to move beyond the enormous wall she had erected in their marriage. His creativity and sense of the dramatic started the process of healing. The work that followed was not easy. But the shower cleansing was the first step. It paved the way to saving their marriage.

CONTENTMENT IN ANY CIRCUMSTANCE

The apostle Paul is another outstanding example of humility. This thoroughly converted man lived a life of dedicated service to Jesus. But his life was anything but easy. He was beaten, robbed, stoned, and imprisoned. Paul could have complained that since he had given so much for Christ, surely Christ could make the way a little easier for him. If anyone was ever entitled to a little extra consideration, surely this man was. But Paul never complained or acted as if he deserved better. He humbled himself, and when he could not change his circumstances, he changed his attitude. In one of his letters he wrote:

> I have learned to be content whatever the circumstances. I know what it is to be in need, and I know what it is to have plenty. I have learned the secret of being content in any and every situation, whether well fed or hungry, whether living in plenty or in want. (Philippians 4:11–12)

There is no way Paul could have reached that point had he held on to a sense of arrogant entitlement. Only people who are truly humble can be content when they are needy. Humility leads to contentment and satisfaction. It spawns a life of thanksgiving rather than disappointment. A humble heart draws people to you. They are repelled by self-centeredness and the arrogance of entitlement.

The following story sums up the difference between self-centered entitlement and humility:

A voyaging ship was wrecked during a storm, and only two of the passengers managed to swim to a small, desertlike island. The two survivors realized they had no other recourse but prayer. However, as an experiment to find out whose prayer was more powerful, they agreed to divide the territory between them and stay on opposite sides of the island.

The first thing they prayed for was food. The next morning, a fruit-bearing tree appeared on the side of the island belonging to the first man. The other man's land remained barren.

Next, the first man prayed for a house, clothes, and more food. On the following day, like magic, all of these things appeared. The second man still had nothing. Finally, the first man prayed for a ship so he could leave the island. In the morning, a ship docked on his side of the island. Unconcerned about the second man, he boarded the ship.

As the ship was about to set sail, the first man heard a voice from heaven booming, "Why are you leaving your companion on the island?"

"My blessings are mine alone, since I was the one who prayed for them," the first man answered. "His prayers were not answered, so it's clear that he does not deserve anything."

"You are mistaken!" the voice rebuked him. "He had only one prayer, which I answered. If not for that prayer, you would not have received any of my blessings."

"Tell me," the first man asked, "what did he pray for that I should owe him anything?"

"He prayed that all your prayers would be answered."

The story expresses a dominant human tendency. We are, by our fallen natures, concerned first with our own needs. We pursue what we want, and when we get it, we feel that we simply got what we were entitled to have. It's only when all our own needs are met, if at all, that we tend to take into consideration the needs of others. Humility inverts this perspective.

But the question is, why would self-centered people who feel a sense of entitlement want to change their perspective? The answer is that it's not likely they will want to change until they hit the wall of isolation and shattered relationships that arrogant entitlement will inevitably bring. At that point, they may be willing to look at alternatives to the way they live.

Of course it will be much better if they can see the wall before they hit it. If what I have written opens their eyes and shows them where they are headed, that could open them to the wisdom of giving humility a try.

Humility will not come easy at first. You must commit yourself to it. It takes practice, but the more you try it, the easier it becomes. The more you try it, the more you begin to reap the rewards of improved relationships and an easing up of that terrible pressure to be right, have more, defend your turf, and constantly war with others in order to have things your way.

Start now. The next time you feel the need to step up, just step back instead. It will get easier each time you try it.

Resentment is toxic! It can eat out your soul like an acid. Resentment also gives up control of your life to the person you resent. We don't realize that when we resent a person for what he has done to us, we do the very opposite of what we want: we allow that person to control us. He becomes a wall that stops us cold, casting a dark shadow on the present and blocking off the future.

chapter four

THE WALL OF JUSTIFIABLE RESENTMENT

No one in his right mind would walk around carrying radio-active plutonium in his pockets. The stuff will make you sick, mutate your genes, and cause you to die a slow, painful death. The good thing about plutonium is that it exists in solid form and is always packaged in protective materials and labeled with warnings. Unfortunately, that is not the case with what I believe is the most dangerous thing people carry around inside their souls. That possession is *justifiable resentment*. It can eat you alive just as surely as plutonium can.

Are you angry about something in your life? Has someone hurt you, and you feel that you have every right to remain angry and bitter toward that person? Have you done something so awful that you cannot forgive yourself? In other words, is there something in the past—either that you did or was done to you—

which has left you feeling bitterness, anger, or resentment that you are convinced is perfectly justifiable?

Perhaps you have buried the event so deeply or covered it so effectively that you no longer think about it. But when you stop and consider your life, you realize you have continued to harbor this hard place in your heart, and you believe that anyone who went through such an experience would feel the same way. If you are carrying around anything like this, it is as dangerous as any radioactive material. It can do more than destroy you; it can eat away at who you are at the deepest levels of your being.

Brushing Aside Petty Resentments

What I am addressing here are not the little irritations that might momentarily upset us from day to day. All of us do quirky things that irritate others. Recently my wife, Misty, and I were driving down the road with our four kids. Our daughter Madeline explained something she had learned in driver's training—an acronym designed to help her remember what to do when changing lanes: SMOG. *S* stands for "turn on your signal," *M* stands for "look into your mirror," *O* stands for "look over your shoulder," and *G* stands for "hit the gas and make the turn."

I responded that I use the GAS method: *G* stands for "gun it," *A* stands for "ask if anyone sees anything in the way," and *S* stands for "slam on the brakes right before I hit someone." Immediately Misty started laughing. Why? It was because I had accurately nailed the driving technique that causes her so much irritation and anguish.

My wife cannot stand the way I drive anything. Whether it's

a car, a boat, or a lawn mower, my driving drives her up the wall. I have come to realize that older men allow women to drive not because they are old but to stay sane. The conflict would drive them crazy.

We all have these petty resentments, but we can easily brush them aside. They are not going to eat away at us if we see them as part of the natural differences we expect to deal with when sharing our lives with others. We all have these minor irritations with others that remain just that: minor irritations we let roll off and learn to live with.

THE ROOTS OF BITTERNESS

The expression *learn to live with* means we adjust to or accommodate the humanity of another person and learn to accept it as part of the reality of being imperfect people. But there is a negative use of the phrase *learn to live with* that actually is more about dying. Learning to live with a toxic resentment is like learning to live with a deadly lump of plutonium in your pocket. Some hurts or affronts go so deep that they implant in our hearts a *root of bitterness*. I appreciate this phrase because it so accurately describes the source of so much of our misery. When we speak of resentment, we are dealing not with a limb that needs to be lopped off or a trunk to be chopped down, but with a root that must be dug out of the ground of our past and destroyed forever.

The Bible addresses this heart problem directly in Ephesians 4:31, where we are told to "get rid of all bitterness, rage and anger." We are not instructed to get rid of all bitterness, *except when* someone has done something really horrible to us. We are not instructed to verify what happened to us as so horrible that we are justified in our resentment. No, we are told simply and clearly to get rid of it.

Why? Because it eats away at us, takes away our drive to fulfill our purposes in life, and taints all our relationships. In short, resentment becomes a huge wall that blocks our lives. It also dishonors God, who has forgiven us of so much and wants us to be willing to forgive others. Job 5:2 reveals that "resentment kills a fool," and we see it happening all the time. When we hold fast to resentment, we either chain ourselves to a past or to a person who produced pain we cannot undo and whom we cannot change. The alternative is to find a way to move on, give up our right to resent, and find a way to forgive. Until we do that, the justifiable resentment will be a wall that is impossible to get past.

Wearing the Offender's Shoes

When people give up their anger long enough to peer into the hearts of others, it can make all the difference in the world and restore relationships that could have remained broken forever. This giving up is not easy—humility and a surrendered heart are required to make it work. But when it does work, the best surprises can happen.

I was speaking at a large conference on getting into the shoes of a person who has offended you. I challenged people who were hurt in the worst ways to do the unimaginable and try to take the side of the person who hurt them, just to see if it would help them move beyond the event and get them over their resentment.

As I was speaking I thought about how this must sound to someone abused as a child by a parent or to a woman whose husband ran off with someone much younger. But I knew that even in those cases, this exercise could unlock their continuing focus on how they were hurt and enable them to move on. The exercise is not intended to justify or rationalize the evil that was done. It is intended to humanize the offender so forgiveness can be more easily rendered. You can't forgive a devil, but you can forgive a person consumed by a sickness.

After I presented this delicate concept, trying not to negate the accurate placement of blame on the perpetrator, a couple approached and poured out their hearts about a tragedy that occurred in their family. They had started a mail-order jewelry business, which did quite well. Their daughter was interested in the business and began working with them right out of college. As the parents progressed in years, they gave her more responsibility in hopes that one day she would take over and they could retire. All seemed to be going well until an annual audit revealed something disturbing. Over the previous two years, three hundred thousand dollars had been taken out of the company.

To the father, this was incomprehensible. He knew where every penny was spent—at least, he thought he did. He called in a group of auditors to investigate. They discovered that the missing money had gone into an account managed by the daughter. The couple's own flesh and blood had embezzled the money from them.

The parents did what they would have done had the criminal been anyone else. They called the district attorney, turned over the evidence, and pressed charges against their daughter. She pleaded no contest and served six months in jail. When she was released, her mother and father told her she was no longer a part of the family. They did not want to see her again.

The daughter made attempts at reconciliation, but to no avail. Her parents saw her as a vicious, ungrateful, and unloving woman who didn't care about them. In their minds she was all bad because she would have to be all bad to betray and steal from her own parents.

But there was a problem. This couple's justifiable resentment toward their daughter was so deep that neither the mother nor the father could sleep. They faced a nightly ritual of tossing, turning, pacing, and just trying to make it through another miserable night. And it continued to get worse. By the time they heard my talk on wearing the shoes of the offender, they were more miserable than they had ever been in their lives.

This couple was moved by my talk. They realized they were carrying a justifiable resentment and held on to their anger because they felt they were entitled to it. When I asked them to step into their daughter's shoes, they did just that. Afterward the father explained that he and his wife now saw her in a totally different light. They came to see her as something other than a criminal who had set out to hurt them. In fact, the father took some responsibility for her desperation. He had paid her about a third of what others in her position made, thinking that she would appreciate the fact that there was that much more in the company when she took over.

As the parents reflected on what their daughter had said when she confessed to the crime, they began to see things from her perspective. She had felt neglected when she was younger. Working, talking about work, and traveling took all her parents' time, and they had none left for her. She said her embezzling became a compulsive action, triggered each time they left her in charge of the operation.

Now the parents could see what she had been trying to explain. She was not justifying what she did as right; she was simply trying to help them see how something so ugly could spring up inside her. She was not blaming them; she was just trying to help them believe she did not hate them. She felt deserving of everything bad that happened to her.

As a result of putting themselves in their daughter's shoes, the parents realized they had treated her too harshly. Their resentment had led them to become vindictive toward her, and they were ready to turn things around.

The couple went home and wrote their daughter a letter, telling her they had made a mistake. They had been too harsh, and they had let their resentment build a wall between them. They wanted her back as their daughter. All was forgiven, and they were ready to start over if she was ready.

It was a dramatic change of heart, and it broke down a huge wall that had isolated them in bitterness and resentment. Even if their daughter did not respond, they had gotten out of their own shoes and into hers and discovered truths they had blocked themselves from seeing. I don't know the result of their letter to their daughter, but I could see that there was already an enormous result in their hearts.

Letting Go of Resentment

In summary, when you hold on to resentment, even if you think it's justifiable, only bad things can result. Resentment is toxic, and it can eat out your soul like an acid. Resentment also gives up control of your life to the person you resent. We don't realize that when we resent a person for what he has done to us, we do the very opposite of what we want: we allow that person to control us. He becomes a wall that stops us cold, casting a dark shadow on the present and blocking off the future.

Of course, we know not to let the daily, ordinary, little, petty irritations that come naturally with any relationship swell into full-blown resentment. What we fail to remember is that we must do the same with the huge wrongs, conflicts, and betrayals. You may never change the person you resent, but getting rid of the resentment will certainly change you. We will explore more about how that can be done in the next section.

Forgiveness: The Key to Overcoming Justifiable Resentment

Without exception we are to forgive, no matter how strongly we feel that the severity of the offense justifies our continued resentment. When Peter wanted to clarify the concept of forgiveness with Jesus, he was thinking that seven times ought to be about enough. But Jesus came up with a calculation of seventy times seven, indicating that the number of times we need to forgive is unlimited (Matthew 18:22). We have a mandate to forgive.

Often we look for any possible loophole to withhold forgiveness, but there is none. We must forgive.

When the hurt is deep, forgiveness can seem too much to ask. Some are unwilling to forgive the persons who hurt them because they believe the abusers deserve the worst. Or they think forgiving lets the perpetrators off scot-free and seems to allow them to think their despicable act was justifiable. Others can't forgive because they simply cannot get over the pain they went through. They continue to relive that pain and are often defined by it. But when they let go, they regain their ability to live healthily in the present and develop lives with purpose for the future.

I have been the victim of offenses that I thought were so great, no one could ask me to forgive them. In one instance, a Christian businessman took from me more than one million dollars in canceled contracts and unfulfilled commitments, all the while acting as if he was full of love and compassion. In another instance, a person in ministry betrayed me after convincing me she could be trusted. In both situations I was astounded at the depth of the pain, and I could not believe, on top of it all, that I had to forgive these people. Anyone could see I was entitled to any amount of anger, rage, resentment, or bitterness. Yet from the very moment each of these hurts was inflicted, I was aware of the task at hand: the need to forgive. Even though I felt the full gamut of negative emotions, I quickly began to let go of the resentment. I knew the longer I held on to it, the more it would hurt me.

The forgiveness was not instantaneous; it took time. I had to work through pain and rage and resentment. I had to work through all the wounds from my childhood these betrayals tapped into. I had to look at my own sinful nature and ability to mess up, and I had to slowly but surely tear down this impassable wall so I could move on with my life. I knew if I held on to resentment, it would become a barrier that would halt my progress. My father taught me always to push ahead and keep going. Take initiative and be responsible. I knew the longer I wallowed in anger and bitterness, the more vulnerable I was to letting this wall of resentment turn my life into something it was not meant to be.

So I forgave in both cases. I forgave, and if any vengeance was appropriate, I let God be the avenger. As I write this I have no malice in my heart toward either of these people. The wall is down. I am free.

To be free from the negative influence and what they did to me, or as some would say, all the things I allowed them to do, I had to do the kind of work I recommend that you do. I had to look at these people through a new lens. I had to try to walk in their shoes. But most of all, I had to grant that they had the right to receive what I received from God: his grace for me and for them. His demand for me to forgive. My awareness of all he had forgiven in my own life.

God's truth led me to believe that no matter what anyone did to me or took away from me, he would restore it. I had hope that even the worst pain could be transformed into something of value. So I began to see these people as tools of God—imperfect tools that he was using to transform my character. Since I personally needed so much work, I could not spare the time or energy to focus on their faults. Gradually I came to see them as no worse than I, and even better in some ways.

Once I looked at these people and what they did through a new lens, I was ready to resolve the issues. I did that by grieving what I had lost, working through the fear of what might lie ahead of me, experiencing the pain, and letting go of its source. I began to heal. And one key to that healing was the support I had from the people who were standing by me. This change of perspective enabled me to remove the wall and move on with my life.

Eventually I was able to refocus my life away from the tragedies I had endured. At that point I began to see more clearly the tragedies of others who had been hurt, and I realized that I was in a better place to help them than I had been before my painful experiences. My biggest setbacks gave me open doors into the hearts of those who had been through the same kinds of betrayals. They were drawn to me, and I had a deeper connection to them than ever.

Refocusing on these similarly hurt people at the right time marked the completion of my healing. This allowed me to feel that none of my pain was wasted. God was using it to help others who were struggling as I had.

PAST HURT, PRESENT PAIN

Many people who seem competent and pulled together are actually basket cases of hurt inside. It is because they are holding on to something horrific that happened years ago that still impacts their lives today. These people live behind walls of resentment, and they think it is justifiable because they cannot see the person who hurt them as deserving forgiveness.

One woman came to me wanting to know how to get some-one to ask for her forgiveness. It was an unusual question. Most people ask how to move past being hurt by someone who has never asked for forgiveness. This woman had been divorced twenty years ago by a husband who had fallen in love with another woman, whom he later married. And now this woman wanted her ex-husband to be remorseful enough to ask for her forgiveness, even after twenty years.

This is a classic example of someone stuck behind the wall of a past hurt. She did not grasp how unusual it was to still need an apology from someone who had not been in her life for such a long time. The wasted opportunities for life and happiness caused by this barrier were incalculable.

I discovered that she experienced the deepest hurt of her child-hood when her father divorced her mother to marry someone else, leaving her feeling uncared for and unloved. Her husband knew of this deep wound and how hard it had been for her to trust any man again. The one thing she had asked of him was not to marry her until he knew beyond a shadow of a doubt that he could be faithful to her for a lifetime. After she had been so cautious, his betrayal was more than she could bear. It was the unforgivable sin she thought no one would ever commit against her.

CLINGING TO MEANINGLESS HOPE

After the divorce, this woman refused to get on with her life. She focused solely on what had been done to her. Her life hit a wall of what she considered justifiable resentment, and she could not get past it. She spent years waiting for his marriage to crash and burn so he would come crawling back.

Well, his marriage did not crash and burn. It stayed intact, and the abandoned woman finally had to face the reality that he would never come back. With that possibility out of the picture, she held on to one thing: the hope of his apology and a request for forgiveness. So she came to me wanting to know how to make that happen.

This woman needed to see that the wall that had stopped her life was not anything her former husband did to her; it was what she was doing to herself. Dwelling on a past she could not change had stopped her life cold. In the beginning the blame for the hurt, if she wanted to blame, could be placed on him. But now the problem was not the husband's affair or the divorce. The problem was her reaction to those events. She had to take the focus off what he did and put it on her response. Otherwise she would keep bumping into that wall of resentment throughout her remaining years.

This woman also needed to be more realistic in the way she thought of her former husband. She needed to drop the perspective that he lived in regret and shame over betraying her. The fact that his second marriage lasted showed that he was not all bad. He had hurt her terribly, but inflicting pain apparently was not a pattern with him. Perhaps he learned from his mistake. Perhaps he regretted having victimized her. It was also possible that he felt he could never live up to her expectations and, in a strange way, freed her to find someone who could.

There were many different ways in which she could view what happened so long ago and what that new perspective could mean to her life today. Until she pulled her head out of her hurt to see that she was stuck behind a wall, she would never be able to forgive and move on. Rethinking the past and changing her perspective on her former husband would not fix her problem, but it could begin the process of getting her unstuck from a past she could not change.

THE PROCESS

Forgiveness is a process rather than an event. I have known people who were hurt so deeply, it took them years to get over their wounds. That is why it is best to start immediately with the process. The first step might be nothing more than the realization that you are clinging to something toxic from the past that you feel justified in holding on to. It helps to realize that those negative feelings are doing nothing to the people who hurt you. To the contrary, you are allowing those feelings to continue the negative impact those people had on your life. You are letting them dominate you. It is time to acknowledge that they have remained the focus of too much of your time and attention. Once you see that, you are in a position to begin to let it go.

I don't know of anything that keeps a person stuck behind a wall more than this feeling of justifiable resentment. It is a cancer on the soul. The bitterness is within *you*, not in the person who hurt you. Your anger may give you an illusion of power, but it actually robs you of power, drains off your potential, and poisons all your relationships. That is why, for your sake, not the sake of the offender, you must begin the healing and forgiving process. Otherwise you risk remaining behind a wall that will hold you in a bitter and wasted life focused on the past, rather than enjoying the present and moving into a brighter future.

One of the most beautiful promises in Scripture is found in these words of Jesus, inviting us to a higher way of living than the world offers.

> Come to me, all you who are weary and burdened, and I will give you rest. Take my yoke upon you and learn from me, for I am gentle and humble in heart, and you will find rest for your souls. For my yoke is easy and my burden is light. (Matthew 11:28-30)

He invites us to come closer to him because he wants to give us something we need. He wants to give us rest. He wants to teach us his gentle and humble ways, which will bring peace to our souls. His way is so much easier and lighter than our own. And his way, his life, is all about forgiveness. So at some point, and I hope that point for you is now, you must courageously move toward giving up your resentment and begin replacing it with forgiveness.

I go back to 1 Peter 4:1 and remind myself that it is when I am ready to suffer that I am ready to stop sinning. Anything, such as a grudge, that causes me to fall short of God's mark is sin. So I can either suffer continually in my sin, or I can suffer temporarily in the process of getting out of it and learning to forgive. When I endure the painful process of letting go of the sin of resentment, I bring down a wall. I enable myself to move away from my need to be in control and move toward allowing God's truth to dominate my life.

If I have no relationships to challenge me, I can remain in complete denial. I can do whatever I want and never have to question whether it is the best thing for me. I can pile up bad habits and resentments until they become walls that block my potential. I can avoid the sharpening value of relationships and surrender to a life that offers the least resistance and the least chance for meaning and purpose.

chapter five

THE WALL OF DISCONNECTED ISOLATION

I don't have any problems relating to people. Really. It's true. I am perfectly at ease and easy to get along with, and I don't ever get irritated, angry, or upset with anyone—*as long as I am alone.* It is amazing just how easy and tranquil life is when I am isolated. You would really like me if you observed me alone.

But the perfection that many of us experience when we are alone and disconnected is an illusion. Life alone is easier, but it is emptier. Isolated from relationships that bring out the inner truth about ourselves, we don't have to face who we really are. That means we remain unaware of the areas in which we need to grow. Stagnation becomes comfortable, and we stop developing the maturity and wisdom God wants for us.

If I have no relationships to challenge me, I can remain in complete denial. I can do whatever I want and never have to question whether it is the best thing for me. I can pile up bad habits and resentments until they become walls that block my potential. I can avoid the sharpening value of relationships and surrender to a life that offers the least resistance and the least chance for meaning and purpose.

Those who settle into this rut often become stuck in it because it becomes so comfortable they view it as the way life was meant to be. In reality it is a barrier to life as it is meant to be.

The Disconnected Life

This wall is a tough one to knock down, climb over, or go around. People who have developed disconnected lives rarely see the need to change. They have made their assessment that the world is unsafe, people are not dependable or worth the trouble, or their own relational skills are inadequate. They accept these beliefs as if they were irrefutable facts and live accordingly. Therefore they don't want to be bothered with the work of seeing things from a different perspective. Nor are they open to the suggestion that their outlook may not be exactly on target.

I know this is true because I spent much of my life with this mind-set. I came by my disconnection tendencies honestly through the bloodlines of my parents. Because my father and mother and older brothers modeled disconnection, it was all I knew from early on. I took the cue and lived as if relationships were optional, something you could take care of after everything else was completed. I could be in a crowd of many and still be isolated and disconnected. I lived inside my head.

If you tend to live inside your head, you have no difficulty understanding the concept. Your life consists mostly of your imagination, and though you may run into people now and then, you have no deep connection to anyone. My internal isolation seemed like the perfect place to live, and it was not easy to see that I had gotten it all wrong. I had built a wall against relationships, and with no one close enough to speak to my heart in a way I would hear, it was hard to see any need to tear it down. It took a lot of pain to wake me up to a different and better way.

For some people, disconnected isolation may be a response to a sense of rejection. They did not choose to be disconnected or isolated, but after experiencing enough rejection and humiliation from family or social contacts, they withdrew behind a wall of isolation as self-protection against further hurt. And it became their way of life.

A few years ago I worked with a woman who joined a women's Bible study. They welcomed her, and she was excited to be in the group. But within four weeks, the group failed to include her in some of their events. Then shortly afterward they asked her to not come back to the meetings.

This kind of thing had happened to the woman before, and such repeated experiences made her a prime candidate for disconnected isolation. But she was not willing to settle for that kind of life. Instead, she realized she had a problem and came to me seeking help.

As we explored the Bible study episode, she began to see that she had been blind to some of her own actions. In the beginning she saw the episode only from the perspective of her needs, her rights, and her mistreatment by those "coldhearted" women. But the fact was, these women had been offended by some of the things she did. They were even more offended when they talked to her about them, and she did not take them seriously. They asked her to come on time, but she never did. It was a disruption they were not willing to tolerate. After she failed to bring her Bible, they requested she do so. In response she brought one the size of Texas, seemingly to mock their request. They did not like the negative way she spoke of her husband. Everything wrong in their marriage was his fault, and the continual negativity was infecting their group's discussions. So they went to her and asked her to change those things they found disruptive or offensive. When she acted as if she did not care, they asked her to leave.

Obviously this woman had been blind to these bad patterns in her life. The women in the group had done her a favor by asking her to change things that others in her life had been afraid to discuss. To her great credit, this woman was open enough to see the truth: She had become a demanding, inconsiderate person who had lost touch with the feelings of others. She had become the center of her world, and all that mattered to her was how she felt. If the women in the group had not confronted her, she might have gone through her whole life offending people, using them to make herself feel good, and rejecting them when they failed to boost her ego. The inevitable rejection this kind of behavior would bring could easily have driven this woman behind a wall of disconnected isolation where no one could again inflict on her the pain of exclusion.

The exploration into the truth about herself was painful, but it led to her making major life changes. Had she continued to see things only in the light of her own perspective, she would have kept running into the wall of rejection. She would never have grown beyond her own self-obsession.

Three Common Disconnectors

Several things commonly cause disconnection from others and lead to isolation. One of the biggest disconnectors is the inability to empathize with another person's pain. Once people sense that you are not sensitive to the reality of their pain, it's likely they will not want to continue or deepen the relationship. This lack of empathy can stem from an internal focus on your own pain or a disregard for the other person's value. You can get so caught up in your own wound that you no longer care about the wounds of others. You can even go to the extreme of evaluating others solely on the basis of how they respond to your wound. You may demand from them the empathy and understanding that you will not give to them.

Another big disconnector may be your being so deeply ingrained in your painful past that you are unable to endure the pain of someone else. You resist getting into their lives because you are afraid it may cause you to break under the load of so much agony. When those experiencing their darkest hour sense that you are avoiding giving them comfort in order to protect your own heart, they walk away to find someone who will care.

Another disconnector may be your neediness. If you experience some kind of continual pain, you may also exhibit a grasping neediness that drives others away. They cannot meet the demands you put on a relationship, so they reject you. Taking a hard, honest look at one's self can help a person in this situation see the problem from a different perspective. The rejected person can come to see himself as a contributor to the problem rather than solely as the victim of abandonment.

HONEST SELF-EVALUATION

We relate in the ways we have been taught or in the ways modeled to us. If that teaching or modeling has not been healthy, we may repeat the same relational errors because they are all we know. We are convinced that what we learned is how relationships are supposed to work.

If we are willing to let some honest, objective persons help us probe and uncover the truth, we may discover that we lack an understanding of our roles in relationships. We may think it is our role to lead when it would be better to cooperate. We may think we are not entitled to express our desires, so we cease to be real in the relationship. This causes the other person to have difficulty respecting us or knowing who we really are. We may find that we are too dominant or too passive, too demanding or too subservient, too self-protective or too revealing. Probing honestly may reveal how the roles we take produce results we do not want.

There are other emotional walls that kill relationships too. I have seen many people who want connection and relationship; yet they endure repeated rejection and have no idea why. They appear to be the perfect candidates for relationship. They love the connection. They want to be vulnerable. But their problem is the neediness I mentioned above. They have unrealistic needs that no one can meet; still they yearn to find someone to meet those unrealistic needs. What seem to be attempts at connection are actually forms of begging—begging for what cannot be supplied by one person.

When needy people look hard and objectively at themselves, they can begin to see their unrealistic demands and their bottomless pit of expectations. It helps if they can also come to see some of the realistic needs of other people. As they reduce their expectations of others to a more realistic and authentic level, they begin to lose their self-focus and replace it with empathy for the hurts of others. Meeting the needs of others, rather than desperately using others to meet their own needs, becomes a point of strong, mutual connection. Relationships can be built on mutual respect and authentic desire for the good of all, rather than being dominated by fear, shame, control, and desperation.

Old views can be hard to give up. But the alternative is to live behind a confining wall that prevents growth and joy. The change doesn't just happen. It's up to you to make the move to connect in deeper ways with others. It is a giant step in getting past the wall and seeing life for what it is meant to be.

Intimacy: The Key to Overcoming Disconnected Isolation

Your first thought may be that this heading is too obvious to have any real meaning. *Well, of course intimacy will overcome disconnected isolation. Duh!* But the problem is that if a person has chosen disconnected isolation, why should he even want to consider intimacy? The very reason he made the choice to disconnect is that intimacy takes work, becomes complex, means vulnerability and pain, and calls for giving up parts of the self that he wants to retain. So why should he bother with changing?

He should bother because his isolation is a wall that will separate him from his full potential—from deep joy and from the way humans are designed to live as relational beings in community with others. Living in isolation in your own created world of the mind may work for a while, but eventually the weight of truth will press the joy out of the isolated life.

Living in relationships helps us to see the truth by broadening our perspectives. We are exposed to another person's point of view, which opens our hearts and minds to new ways of looking at reality. As we relate to people who care for us and reveal themselves to us, we begin to see our own flaws. We begin to make adjustments, both minor and major, that help us grow closer to the beings we are intended to become.

One of the difficult things about entering into intimacy is that if we have been hurt in the past, intimacy is the opposite of what we want. Who can blame a woman who was abused early in life for defining all relationships according to that abuse? Who can blame someone who was abandoned emotionally or physically for believing that all relationships end in abandonment? It would be only natural to hunker down and protect oneself after being so cruelly treated as a child. From that position the world and people would seem very unsafe. We think our greatest need is protection from further damage, but it's not. Our real need is safe connection to help us view the world in a different way.

One young woman came to me with a problem connecting to men. If there were ten levels in relationships, she could reach only about level four. At that point she guarded and protected herself, limiting her vulnerability to hurt.

As we discussed her life experiences, it became obvious why she had difficulty relating to men at the deeper levels. First of all, she was adopted, so she carried a vague sense that the first man in her life had not accepted her. Then the parents who adopted her were in constant conflict and eventually divorced when she was in her late teens. She had a loving relationship with her adoptive father, but she always felt that if he had been stronger, he could have prevented the divorce. Throughout the parents' growing marital conflict, he was guarded in his reaction to her mother, even though the mother was unfaithful, angry, and extremely disconnected. In other words the one man she connected with could go only so deep in his own intimate relationships. Thus the daughter, sensing his limited ability to relate, held him responsible for the home breakup. He was the second male to fail her at some level.

As we processed this woman's history, it became evident that her loving relationship with her adoptive father had helped her to be comfortable with men and enjoy many healthy male friendships. But the real or imagined abandonments and disappointments inflicted by him and her birth father had erected a wall of caution that blocked these relationships from going deeper.

Once she realized the past was blocking her relationships,

she went back to the man in her past—her adoptive father—and started sharing her heart and asking him deeply probing questions. She came to understand the harshness with which he was raised and the emotional desert of his family life. As their talks continued, she found that she no longer held a grudge and expected less and less from him while enjoying their times together more than ever.

Then, as she dated men, she quit looking at each as the potential life partner she sought. Instead, she accepted each experience as something to enjoy simply for what it was—a chance to get to know another person. She began to put something into the life of the other person while learning to share more freely and trust more. She kept a diary to assist her in plotting how deeply she felt she was sharing her feelings and how vulnerable she was when she was on a date.

This new way of approaching relationships lessened her anxiety with the men she dated. She no longer worried about her lack of relational depth; she was doing something about it. She did not waste time worrying about whether he liked her. Yet when she was with someone who seemed safe, she practiced being vulnerable. Essentially she stretched her vulnerability muscles and learned to connect on deeper levels.

While she did these exercises, she was setting an example with the guys she dated. It was more than just all about her. It became about those young men also. She became very good at sharing without appearing needy or too invasive.

This woman's wall was seeing men as undependable—her assumption that all relationships with men result in abandonment or disappointment. She changed her view and her wall tumbled down. She did not ignore her past; she worked with it. She uncovered the truth and used the results to knock down a wall and enable her growth. Pretty soon she was living a lifestyle of intimate connection.

Your Rights versus What Is Right

If you have grown up not knowing how to develop intimate relationships, then you can blame your isolation on your weirdo parents, who just never taught you about intimacy, or who gave you negative models or experiences. But the fact is, what they might have taught you was how to perfectly destroy intimate relationships. Whether it was stepping back and withdrawing or stepping up and attacking, you learned from them crummy ways of relating, and that gives you the perfect right to continue relating in that way.

In other words, you have the *right* (or should we call it an excuse?) to remain behind that wall you blame someone else for building. But if you want to live a healthy and satisfying life, at some point you must give up that right and reach out to others for relationships. Give up your rights for what is truly right, and you will find that you made a good trade.

Dictator-Doormat Theology

Sadly it is not only our experiences from childhood that can put us behind walls of disconnected isolation. Sometimes religious teaching can do it. I don't mean authentic Christian teaching; Christ did not live in isolation. He connected with the outcasts, the lowly, and the unlikely. He had a group of men around him whom he loved and accepted with all their flaws. He taught how to be in relationship. Clearly, disconnected isolation does not come from following Christ.

But there are erroneous teachings spoken in the name of Christ that lead to isolation. None of those teachings is more distorted than the way some twist the meaning of *submission*.

Submission is falsely taught as the attitude women should adopt toward men. It puts men in a one-up position and entitles them to trample on women and treat them as lesser beings. This distortion has produced many marriages where men are totally isolated at the top of the relationship and women are walled out down below. This prohibits each spouse from connecting and experiencing a fulfilling relationship with the other. Most of this teaching starts and stops with one verse: "Wives, submit to your husbands as to the Lord" (Ephesians 5:22).

On the surface, that sounds pretty clear-cut. It enables a man to act as a dictator, trampling over his doormat wife, all in the name of the Scriptures. It is a license to kill every marital opportunity for intimate connection. But anyone who takes that course is using truth in an untruthful way. This verse may be Exhibit A as evidence for crimes committed in the name of God. And it is all because men take this scripture out of context and use it to keep their wives "in their place." And they also use it to avoid self-examination.

All you have to do is back up one verse, and you find the

proper context in which Paul gave the command: "Submit to one another out of reverence for Christ" (Ephesians 5:21).

What Paul was teaching here is a *mutual submission* that builds connection. In the context of mutual submission, Paul elaborated with the principle of wives submitting to husbands, which is her part in fostering the marital connection. Wives submitting to husbands is a good thing in the context of *mutual* submission.

From Mutuality to Intimacy

If the thought still lingers that it seems unfair of Paul to speak first of mutual submission and then single out the wives for an additional admonition to submit, read on to verse 25. There you will find balance, for in that verse the man is singled out for special responsibility to the woman: "Husbands, love your wives, just as Christ loved the church and gave himself up for her."

That passage sure puts the kibosh on the dictator-doormat arrangement. Husbands are charged to actually *sacrifice* themselves for their wives. Then finally in verse 33 the concept of submission in relationship concludes with this nicely balanced statement: "However, each one of you also must love his wife as he loves himself, and the wife must respect her husband."

Throughout these verses Paul describes a mutuality that builds connection and intimacy. If there is no mutuality in a relationship, there is no intimacy. Men who cling to the dictator-doormat concept of one-way submission tend to have difficulty looking at things in a new light. They have placed themselves in a position of power, and power can be addictive. Thus men can become deeply entrenched and invested in their views.

If this describes you or someone you love, you might want to read *Every Man's Marriage*. My name is on the book as co-author, but it is actually the story of Fred and Brenda Stoeker and how they reestablished their marriage on solid biblical principles. More important, it is the story of how Fred completely changed his view of marriage, his wife, and all women.

I will close this section with three verses. The first reads, "Anyone who loves another brother or sister is living in the light and does not cause others to stumble" (1 John 2:10 NLT).

A married man or woman living in the same house but isolated is causing the other to stumble. Rather than withdrawing into a life of disconnected isolation, you must do what you can to rebuild the bridge to your spouse's heart. If you are single, make sure you are single for some reason other than a fear of vulnerability. Look hard at anything that may be a wall keeping you stuck in old patterns that are not getting you where you want to go.

Finally, without comment I close this chapter with two important, self-evident relational truths from Scripture:

> Let us therefore make every effort to do what leads to peace and to mutual edification. (Romans 14:19)

> Be completely humble and gentle; be patient, bearing with one another in love. (Ephesians 4:2)

It is so easy to be blind to the reality of our own lives. We need people and truth to mirror for us who we are and what we need to do to get on with our lives. You will keep bumping into walls until you open your eyes to the truth.

chapter six

THE WALL OF OF BLIND IGNORANCE

My wife and I love watching a show that is full of miraculous change every week. It may surprise you that I'm not talking about some lofty, educational program on the History Channel or Animal Planet. Our show is *What Not to Wear*, and we love it. If you always flip past this show, thinking it doesn't quite measure up to your elevated level of taste, let me describe it to you. A friend or family member nominates someone to be on the show who has no clue how to dress. If this person accepts, a film crew captures the fashion disaster wearing various outlandish, tasteless, ill-suited, or inappropriate clothes. Almost all of these people believe they have a great sense of style. They tell how they choose their clothes and believe they alone know what is best for them.

It is amazing how these people tend to highlight, rather than camouflage, the worst parts of their bodies. So often a woman on the show looks very nice except for, say, a huge midriff. And sure enough, low-slung pants and a cropped top show off that belly. I yell at the screen, "You have to cover that up!" But for some reason she feels that her style or identity means she must accentuate this most disproportionate area of her body. Why? I have no clue.

What interests me most about this show is watching these people give up their old attitudes and start to see themselves in different lights. The show's hosts, Clinton and Stacy, show them what they are doing wrong, tell them why, and suggest new ways of dressing. Some argue and go into the new clothes kicking and screaming, but when they actually become willing to try the hosts' sense of style, they eventually see the light. They realize they have grown comfortable with some pretty awful duds. Their own vision has become skewed, and in the process of change, they begin to build on the strengths of their bodies and minimize the weaknesses. Often tears are shed at the results of these dramatic makeovers, and generally we are crying too. (Okay, *I* am crying too.)

Knowing You Need Help

Of course, this is a powerful metaphor for all of us who need to make internal changes regarding the fashions of our internal worlds. We wear stuff that has been in the closets of our obsessive minds far too long. We need to replace these old clothes with a new wardrobe of hope and recovery. But often we don't realize that need any better than the victims on *What Not to Wear*.

One night Clinton made a profound statement regarding his guests' approach to style: "Sometimes you don't know you *need* help until you get help." I saw instantly that this statement had a much broader application than just to clothes. I wished I had said it first. Like the guests on *What Not to Wear*, we sometimes think we have it all together. We don't realize we need help until we open our lives to *receiving* help. Then we discover all the awful stuff that has been hanging in our mental closets. We need to replace these ill-fitting and distorted rags with a fresh, new wardrobe of hope and recovery.

As long as we remain in the same routine, not allowing new people to speak truth into our lives, not trying on new ways of living or looking at ourselves, we will continue to miss the best of what God has for us.

The reality is, we all have blind spots when it comes to seeing ourselves. Strangely, when looking at other people's problem areas, we tend to have twenty-twenty vision. I can tell you exactly how other people ought to be raising their kids, pointing out every little flaw in their techniques. But when it comes to my own child rearing, I am blind to those same things. I just don't see my own flaws very clearly.

To some degree or another, we all have personal blind spots that keep us from perceiving the truth accurately. Helen Keller once said that the saddest thing in life is a person who has sight but is blind. Ouch! Too often we are blind to what others plainly see—our defects and areas that need work.

THE LOG AND THE SPECK

Jesus' famous example of taking out the enormous log protruding from one's own eye before attempting to remove the speck of sawdust from the eye of another illustrates a common form of blindness. I saw an example of this the day I received a phone call from a man who had amazing twenty-twenty vision when it came to the faults of his wife, but when it came to seeing his own faults, the man was blind as a bat.

His wife was withholding sex from him, and this was a terrible wrong. It had been three months since he last had sex with her, and for a man who wanted sex every day, that was an eternity. He knew his rights. He even took out the Bible and showed her how wrong she was, pointing out the biblical mandate for a woman not to withhold sex from her husband. For three months he asked for sex and then demanded she perform her wifely duties for him, but she adamantly refused.

From me he wanted to know how much time he needed to give his wife before he was entitled to divorce her and marry a woman who would have sex with him. He was ready to pull out of the relationship because, after all, in withholding sex from him, she was going against God.

THE OTHER SIDE OF THE BED

I wondered what was going on in the relationship to drive this woman to the far side of the bed. Rarely does a woman just up and inform her husband that she is finished with sex, and there will be no more from her. I knew that something was missing from his story—something he was apparently blind to seeing.

I asked him to step back and, to the best of his ability, slip over to her side of the bed and see the situation from her perspective. What possible reason could she have for withholding sex?

After a bit of hedging, he finally unfolded the story of conflict in their marriage over his struggle with alcohol. It turned out that this sexually demanding man was an alcoholic who had experienced five years of sobriety through attendance at Alcoholics Anonymous meetings. But he stopped attending when he felt that he no longer needed the program. When he subsequently relapsed, he reembraced his right to drink.

His wife had not withheld sex when he was sober or even when he first began to drink again. But as his alcoholism grew more troublesome, she told him that things could not stay the same if he did not get help. When he refused to get that help, she refused to be sexual with him until he got sober. He was completely blind to her feelings and her reasons for refusing sex. All he could see plainly was the Bible passage that says a woman should not withhold sex from her husband.

Using Truth in Untruthful Ways

The scripture this man focused on to get his way is found in 1 Corinthians 7:3–5.

> The husband should fulfill his marital duty to his wife, and likewise the wife to her husband. The wife's body does not belong to her alone but also to her husband. In the same way, the husband's body does not belong to him alone but also to his wife. Do not deprive each other except by mutual consent and for a time, so that you may devote yourselves to prayer. Then come together again so that Satan will not tempt you because of your lack of self-control.

As we can see by reading this scripture, the man had a technical point. But he was blindly ignorant of the ultimate point. The truth he needed to see was that his wife felt used and abused as an object to gratify his self-centered desires while he refused to get help for his drinking problem and become the man she hoped she had married. He was using truth in an untruthful way. He was using it to manipulate her into compliance while blindly turning away from his responsibility for his own life. He was blind to the fact that he was a fallen husband who did not have the right to demand anything until he got his act together.

Learning to See the Real Truth

I invited this man to open his heart to a truth he had not previously seen. I presented to him a passage of Scripture I thought was far more relevant to his situation than the one to which he clung. The passage is the one we looked at earlier from the fifth chapter of Ephesians:

Husbands, love your wives, just as Christ loved the church and gave himself up for her to make her holy, cleansing her by the washing with water through the word, and to present her to himself as a radiant church, without stain or wrinkle or any other blemish, but holy and blameless. In this same way, husbands ought to love their wives as their own bodies. He who loves his wife loves himself. After all, no one ever hated his own body, but he feeds and cares for it, just as Christ does the church—for we are members of his body. "For this reason a man will leave his father and mother and be united to his wife, and the two will become one flesh." This is a profound mystery—but I am talking about Christ and the church. However, each one of you also must love his wife as he loves himself, and the wife must respect her husband. (vv. 25–33)

I pointed out that it is not too easy for a wife to respect a man who refuses to quit drinking yet demands sex. I asked him to open his mind to seeing his life as his wife saw it. Early on she saw him showing signs of great hope, only to spiral back down into drunkenness and misery. Rather than having a husband willing to work on his problem and honor her with his humility, he arrogantly and selfishly demanded sex. He wanted a physical home run, but when it came to meeting her deeper relational needs, he had not even made it to first base.

I told him that in most cases like his, a woman would simply walk out the door or indulge in an affair. But his wife had not done that. She had stayed with him in hopes that one day he would love her so much, he would clean up his act and be a man she could again respect and admire.

I told him it was up to him to take off the blinders and make a move toward seeing the truth. He could pick up a phone and find out where the next AA meeting was, then call his wife and tell her he would be home late because he was going to the meeting in order to get his life back on track. I explained that if he made this move, I didn't think her unwillingness to have sex would continue to be a problem. Seeing the truth and acting on it would bring down that wall he had built in their bed.

Keep Me from Lying to Myself

Psalm 119:29 issues a plea to God that we all need to echo: "Keep me from lying to myself" (NLT). We all do it. Even when we don't lie to ourselves overtly, we keep busy enough to avoid looking at the true reality of a situation. That is why we continually need to check our vision by relying on the objectivity of those who know us. So often we are ignorant of our own blind spots. In some cases we don't fully grasp the reality of our lives because we have no one willing to tell us the truth about ourselves. In other cases we blind ourselves to the truth we should see so we won't have to go through uncomfortable changes. We are all blind in some ways, and the only way we will see reality is to take off the blinders, allow others to speak truth to us, and allow the truth of God's Word to seep into our lives.

The prophet Isaiah addressed the people of his day, hoping to shake them up so they would listen to truths from which they had turned away. He upbraided them for their empty religious ritualism, urged them to turn from the idols they were worshipping, and warned them of the coming downfall of the kingdom if they did not change. He could just as easily have been talking to us today:

> Bring out the people who are blind,
> even though they have eyes,
> And the deaf, even though they have ears.
> (Isaiah 43:8 NASB)

People then, like people now, were blind to the reality of their lives, not seeing what was really going on and not hearing those who were trying to open their eyes by challenging their ways of thinking. When we are caught up in our own world, seeing things the way we want to see them, it is hard to see the truth about what we are doing wrong.

We tend to be like the man who took his wife into a fine art gallery. The man considered himself an expert on fine art. As they entered the lobby, he looked at the image hanging there and, in his arrogant manner, began to critique it. "First of all, that frame is not even fit for a fine painting. Second, the subject is not worthy to be in a painting. He is lifeless, drab, and sour looking."

His wife interrupted, "Honey, that is not a painting. That is a mirror."

It is so easy to be blind to the reality of our own lives. We need people and truth to show us the mirror of who we are and what we need to do to get on with our lives. You will keep bumping into walls until you open your eyes to the truth.

Obedience: The Key to
Overcoming Blind Ignorance

It would be natural to think the key to overcoming blind ignorance is knowledge, but that is not the case. The key is obedience. To understand why this is true, there is no better explanation than what we find in the Bible. To know God's will we have to do more than just read about it; we have to do what he tells us to do. John 8:31–32 tells us if we *follow* the teachings of Christ, we will come to know the truth. We speak of Bible reading as if it were, of itself, a great virtue. But reading the Bible is meaningless if you don't put into practice what you read. *Head* knowledge is not *real* knowledge. We come to know the truth only when we act on it. That's when truth becomes part of us and sets us free.

We read the truth and incorporate it into our lives. We read it and respond by doing the right thing. Acting on truth removes the walls we bump into because truth leads us past those walls into wide-open vistas of reality. All truth is from God, and truth conforms us to the way he created us to live. Because he loves us, he created us to live in ways that produce the most satisfying, joyful, loving, and harmonious lives possible. Live your life in any other way, and you will continue to walk into walls, blind in your ignorance of what put those walls in your way and how to get past them. As Jesus said, "You will know the truth, and the truth will set you free" (John 8:32).

Acting on the Truth You See

I don't know of anyone who sees truth more clearly than my friend Brad, who is a Newport Beach policeman. Brad is one of the greatest men walking the face of the planet. He lives the Christian life as few people I have known. A loving husband and father who makes great decisions, Brad has led his family out of a tiny condo into a spacious and beautiful home—all on a policeman's salary. If you knew Brad, I am sure you would respect him as much as I do. Years ago I bought him the pistol he carries. He named it Steve. So you criminals had better beware of Brad and Steve.

One of the reasons Brad does so well in his private life is because the way he functions on the job has seeped into his home. He makes good decisions because he is able to see the truth in the context of the whole picture. Should Brad want to have an easy shift when on patrol, all he would have to do is stay in one place, not look around, not notice what people are doing, drink coffee, then punch out at the end of the shift. If he worked that way, he would never get involved with a conflict or be bothered with filling out a lot of paperwork because he made an arrest or wrote a ticket. His life would be easy. But it would not be obedient to the truth.

Many of us go through life looking for the easy path. We look the other way. We don't get involved. We don't trouble ourselves to see the difficult things we need to do. And this often leads to real tragedy and ruined lives.

Among the saddest stories I have heard are those from daughters who were abused by their fathers. That alone is sad enough, but when the stories involve mothers who knew it was happening and looked the other way, the sadness is profound. One woman said she turned a blind eye and did nothing because it took the pressure off her as a wife. Had she acted on the truth she had known, she would have felt compelled to do what she did not want to do. Instead, she retained her willful blindness and sacrificed her daughter for her own relief.

STOP LOOKING AT THE TOPS OF YOUR SHOES

If you find yourself in the midst of something you know is not right and decide to look the other way, you are not being obedient to the truth. You must start thinking as Brad did. It is your duty as an adult to look around, to be aware, to see. What about those areas in your own life you have neglected because you refused to look at them? Your willful blindness has become a wall, and in order to move into freedom, those problem areas must no longer be overlooked. You have a job to do for yourself, your family, and your friends. You must stop staring at the top of your shoes and look hard at those truths you do not want to see.

Your problem areas may be financial, they may be health related, they may involve your kids or spouse or the person you are dating. You must become the policeman of your life, and that means you must stop turning a blind eye to your problems. You must begin to look and listen and notice everything, especially the bad stuff that can pile up and become a wall.

SEEING THE TRUTH BENEATH THE SURFACE

One thing Brad cannot do as a police officer is take everyone or everything at face value. Since he deals largely with people who create problems, he has to assume the people he challenges are motivated to hide a big chunk of reality.

When he stops a driver who was weaving into oncoming traffic and asks if he has been drinking, it would make his life easier simply to always accept what the driver says. If the driver insists that he had only a tiny glass of wine with dinner, Brad could take him at face value and say, "Okay, in that case you can go on. Have a nice day. Sorry to bother you." But that easy response is not going to save lives and get drunk drivers off the road. So Brad hears what the person says, but he assumes it might not be the whole picture. The driver might have had only a couple of glasses of wine. But there is a good chance, based on his erratic driving, that the two glasses of wine were on top of a six-pack of beer or a slew of mixed drinks. So Brad goes to the trouble of seeing if there is substance behind the driver's claim. Perhaps he is not drunk. Perhaps he was just momentarily distracted. To ascertain the truth, Brad observes the driver's speech pattern, listening for slurs and inconsistencies, and eventually requires him to prove he is sober enough to drive by taking a couple of standard tests. Brad's awareness leads to action, and the action leads to a safer world. He seeks to find the truth, and then he acts in obedience to it.

We all need to be more like Brad. We need to be aware of what is going on around us. We must look not only on the surface, which may not reveal the real truth, but we must take the painful step of probing beneath the surface until we uncover the problems that block our lives. The obedient mind is able to see because it wants to see, and it thrives on being aware. The obedient mind seeks to see reality and intervenes where appropriate. Responsible action for self, family, and friends replaces irresponsible, willful blindness. Concentration heightens. Focus is sharpened, and the substance of thoughts and feelings changes. Out of this new mind-set of awareness, a whole new way of living emerges. A way that is obedient to the truth. It doesn't happen quickly or easily, but at some point people who are obedient to truth will wake up and realize they have taken charge of their lives. They now see the world through the lens of truth, and they act on it in responsible ways. When that happens, walls fall down.

SUMMARY OF OUR COMMON WALLS

If you want to benefit from the rest of this book, you must sacrifice some baggage that may have become dear to you. You will have to

- release your stubborn resistance
- let go of your arrogant entitlement
- put away your justifiable resentments
- come out of your disconnected isolation
- refuse to live in blind ignorance

In their places, you must pick up

- willingness to change
- humility
- forgiveness
- intimacy
- obedience

Fill your soul with these things, which can help you to rethink the most difficult aspects of your life. Become willing to try a new way to live. Humble yourself before others so you can exist on a level plane with them. Begin the process of forgiveness by trying to understand the traumas in the lives of those who have hurt you. Connect mutually with those you love so you can experience deeper intimacy in relationships.

Do these things, and you will find that you have laid down a burden of heavy, dragging weight. And what you have picked up instead is no burden at all. You will be following the path of Jesus, and when you become obedient to him, you will learn what he meant when he said, "For my yoke is easy and my burden is light" (Matthew 11:30).

It's like exchanging lead for helium. Instead of bearing a painful, heavy load that leaves you earthbound behind walls, you can now soar over them.

Reaching a new perspective that gets you unstuck from your past is a combination of humility, awareness, spiritual focus, and grace. These four components can provide a corrective lens through which you can see anything from the past or in the present. They can help you get past your walls and move on toward a bright future.

chapter seven

GETTING UNSTUCK

Almost every day I come across a new study in *USA Today;* the *New York Times; O, The Oprah Magazine;* or *Reader's Digest* confirming that the state of our minds and hearts has a lot to do with our health. Angry people have heart attacks. Depressed people have low immunity. Anxious people pump glucocorticoid hormones through their bodies, which wears them out from all the stress. In all my years of reading and research, I have never found it suggested that if we hold on to our grudges, live our lives full of fear, or slump around waiting for the next shoe to drop, our health will improve greatly. None of these actions is good for us, and if we hang on to them, they will keep us stuck behind walls and undo our well-being.

When we find ourselves stuck behind the walls we build, getting unstuck is not as simple as we would like it to be. Focusing on the negatives wears us down and deteriorates our health. It causes us to retreat, isolate, and become inactive. The resulting inertia leads to darker feelings and obsessions of the mind. Worry and physical complaints begin to dominate our thinking and sicken our bodies. Not only are we stuck; we have depleted the very resources we need to get unstuck.

Doctors are not always helpful. They tell us that things must change, they put us on diets we hate and can't follow, or they instruct us to exercise in ways that we lack the will to follow. But if we are stuck emotionally, we do not have the ability to change so dramatically, even if we want to.

THE BENEFITS OF LIVING IN THE PAST

One reason it is hard to change our perspectives is that when we are stuck in the past, we actually discover certain benefits to living that way. These benefits are hard to give up. One benefit is that we do not have to participate fully in life because we see ourselves as damaged goods. Another benefit is that by focusing on the past, we justify not taking the risks involved in new relationships—relationships that might not turn out well and might end in hurt.

Perhaps the most common benefit of staying stuck in the past is that the hurts we experienced long ago become the excuse for everything done in excess—overeating, overdrinking, overspending, or over-anything. All our overindulgence in the present is simply a result of that sad thing in our past. We see our lives as permanently tainted by the event, which has the benefit of removing from us the responsibility for our dysfunctional behavior.

Change Your Thoughts, Change Your Life

When we are willing to change our thinking, we become able to see that our walls are created not really by the trauma of the past but by our reaction to it. Our problem is what we have done *to ourselves* in response to the original trauma. More than we realize, it is our thinking about events of the past that keeps us unhealthy, unhappy, and stuck behind walls. So it doesn't take a rocket scientist to conclude that if we want to get unstuck and move past those walls, we need to change the way we think about the past. Almost always, we who are stuck behind walls have developed a distorted, inaccurate view of the past. Even if our view is not altogether inaccurate, it is often distorted in a way that magnifies its impact on us and gives it importance far beyond what it deserves.

This change in thinking requires that we see the picture through a new frame. Like a movie director who forms with his fingers a little rectangle through which to view a camera shot, we need to form an accurate frame through which we can view the past and see a true picture of it. Putting a new frame on the past will not change it, but it can change our outlook on the events that traumatized us. This change could get us unstuck and started down a new and brighter path. The knowledge of our past life will still be there, but its negative impact will be wiped out.

Seeing the past through a new frame involves both looking at yourself and at the people who have hurt you, seeing everything in a more accurate perspective. Let's start with you.

People who have let circumstances, hard blows, traumas, or disappointments build walls in their lives commonly tend to develop a low, defeatist view of themselves. Such views are always inaccurate. Furthermore they can become excuses that keep you from trying to do better. In almost every case of this kind of thinking, reframing can both produce a more accurate picture of the truth and remove the wall that has kept you from moving forward.

How Jesus Corrected People's Perspectives

Jesus, the central figure of Christianity, often removed walls by putting a true perspective on the realities of people's lives. When some thought a widow's tiny gift was worthless because it had virtually no monetary value, Jesus led them to see the gift in terms of sacrifice, which showed it to be one of the largest gifts ever given in honor of God. When men were ready to stone a woman caught in adultery, Jesus forced them to see the woman in light of their own sins and indiscretions. When he showed them that her reality was also *their* reality, not one could pick up a stone.

The Sermon on the Mount is a guide to seeing life from a true perspective. It invites us to see people and events in a different light. It says the powerless are often the greatest. Sufferers will be given special attention rather than being treated as outcasts.

In one of the most radical statements of all time, Jesus taught that "many who are first will be last" (Matthew 19:30). He was implying that a lot of religious leaders who enjoy much honor here will receive none in heaven. It's no wonder they crucified him! Jesus produced a radical shift in thinking that turned the world upside down. Now, two thousand years later, millions are seeing the world and themselves through the corrective frame of his teachings.

SEEING YOURSELF FROM A NEW PERSPECTIVE

Let's look briefly at how you might begin to get a truer perspective on your own life. When you are stuck behind walls, you hold on to thoughts and feelings that distort your outlook and damage your health. Events of the past may have you stuck in thinking your problems are all caused by the actions of others, whereas they might be caused by reactions of your own that are not at all based on truth. A radical shift in your perspective could enable you to view the past more accurately and see the truth in a way that frees you from your wall. Here are some examples of inaccurate thinking followed by a more accurate perspective:

- I have a crummy set of genes, and therefore I am always going to be sick, just as my parents were.

  No matter what genes were handed down to me, I can make a difference in my health with my attitude. I can eat better than my parents taught me to eat. I can exercise wisely. I can find new ways to cope with stress other than worrying, drinking, eating, stewing, or any of the things I watched them do.

- I have always been a bit down at every stage of my life.

  The reason I have been down is that I have always looked on the dark side of things. I can start looking at the bright side. I have lived disconnected from others and prevented myself from experiencing the happiness of relationships. I can join groups where I will be cared for and loved. If I need medication, I can become willing to take it. If I need to stop drinking, I can do that. I can change the way I view my life and the lives of others. I can make a difference in how I feel and the level of health at which I function.

- My loneliness is what keeps me locked up and in bed so much.

  I am lonely because I have been waiting for people to show they care about me, even though I have not shown that I care about them. I can reverse that. I can get out of this bed, and I can go and see someone. I can pay a visit to someone in worse shape than I am, and I can pick up my spirits by picking up theirs. Rather than wait for someone to reach out to me, I can reach out to others.

  Even if I can't get out of bed, I can pick up the phone and call. I can pick up a pen and write a letter that might change someone else's day or week. And if I am unable to carry out what I intend to do, I can ask for support from someone who can help me do what I cannot do on my own. I don't have to be like this.

These changes in outlook do not solve anything, but they lead to the next step of resolving, which we will address in the next chapter. They are beginnings, not the end. They enable you to get unstuck, and you cannot move beyond your wall unless you take that first step of getting unstuck.

SEEING THOSE WHO HURT YOU FROM A NEW PERSPECTIVE

When it comes to developing a truer perspective on those who have hurt you in the past, it might help to put yourself in the position of those who have been sexually abused. What happened to you may have been something quite different. But if you want to begin the process of healing, like the victims of sexual abuse, you too must go through the painful process of seeing the person who harmed you in a different light. This will be painful, but it will lead you to freedom.

The first step is to become willing to give up the old frame in which you have viewed this person. Here are some components you might have used in creating that frame:

- The person who hurt me is all bad.

- The person has no regrets.

- The person is beyond redemption.

- The person deserves nothing.

- The person has nothing of value to offer this world.

- The person is hopeless.

- The person should say he or she is sorry before I move on.

- The person is responsible for my misery.

You can keep this frame firmly in place, but I can assure you that no matter how terribly this person treated you, this view that shows him or her to be utterly evil and beyond redemption in every respect is certainly inaccurate. It you retain this distorted view, you will remain stuck behind your wall. If you want to move on with your life, you must be willing to look at other ways in which that person and his actions could be viewed.

I had to do this very thing. I had been betrayed in the worst of ways. Unfaithfulness and infidelity set me back in every area of my life. There seemed to be little or no remorse on the part of the woman who did it. I actually wanted her to die. I knew I was making progress when I only wanted her to experience a chronic illness. But then something began to happen.

At first I began to see that just because I had not committed a betrayal, I was not morally superior. I also am a sinner. Suffering betrayal did not provide me with a pedestal from which I was entitled to point the finger for the rest of my life. I had to come down off that pedestal, and when I did, things began to change. I went from wanting the worst for that woman to not really caring what happened to her. And then, within a few years, I was at a place where I could say I actually wanted good things for her. So I have had to go through the process of giving up my former view and attitude toward this woman so I could move past my focus on how she had hurt me.

That is what we need to do; now let's look at how to do it. I will show you step by step how to develop an altogether new perspective on those who have hurt you in the past.

THE FIRST STEP TOWARD A NEW PERSPECTIVE

The first step in gaining a truer perspective on the past is your own personal stance of humility. Like me, you may have climbed up on a moral pedestal and thought you were entitled to finger pointing. But as Paul tells us, that idea is far from reality: "For everyone has sinned; we all fall short of God's glorious standard" (Romans 3:23 NLT).

Every one of us has messed up, and we are all fellow strugglers. When we acknowledge this fact, we take away our entitlement to blame and shame. We take the focus off the evil done to us and put more emphasis on the reality of our own struggles as fallible human beings. We realize we would have made mistakes even if no one had hurt us. Even without this particular hurt that has become a wall for us, life still would not have been a piece of cake because we, in and of ourselves, would have sinned and messed it up in other ways. People would have hurt us in different ways. In other words, all the trouble and pain in our lives cannot be blamed on a person who neglected, abused, and hurt us. It happens to all people all the time. Being hurt does not make us unique. We must humbly see ourselves as we really are. We are not morally superior to the one who hurt us.

THE SECOND STEP TOWARD A NEW PERSPECTIVE

The second step we must take to gain a truer perspective is based on a concept found in Galatians 5:16. Here we are instructed to do exactly the opposite of what feels most normal: "So I say, let the Holy Spirit guide your lives. Then you won't be doing what your sinful nature craves" (NLT).

Those of us who have been hurt tend to crave revenge. Our flesh and our instincts tell us to get even and see that the offending person is punished as harshly as possible. If we were controlled solely by emotion and instinct, we would take steps to satisfy our longing for vengeance.

We do not have to live as slaves to our emotions and instincts, because we can tap into a greater power that can control these troublesome impulses. If we want a life of peace, it is important that we find that power and access it. If we want to get unstuck and move past our walls, we must come to the place where we treat people better than our abuser treated us. The power of the Holy Spirit allows us to do that.

While no one really understands the Trinitarian nature of God, his Holy Spirit is his relational Person. The Holy Spirit empowers us to do what no one could do without supernatural intervention. We can live above the raw emotions and instincts that make up our troublesome natural selves.

Depending on the power of the Holy Spirit means, rather than reacting emotionally to anything done to me, I can maintain my composure. I can let a little time pass and then respond in a more loving way. The Holy Spirit enables me to let go of things others would hold on to.

When I incorporate humility with living by the power of the Holy Spirit, a chunk of bitter concrete starts to break off those walls I build to protect me. I don't need those walls because I am walking in supernatural power with humility. I do not focus so much on the bad that has happened to me. Instead, I begin to look ahead. I begin to see the person who hurt me as one who needs what I have, and I can begin praying for his healing.

When I do that, I replace the earthly desire for revenge with a spiritual mind-set that needs no revenge. The next time you are tempted to become enraged, remind yourself that you have a power within that can conquer anything.

The Third Step toward a New Perspective

The third step toward gaining a truer perspective on the past is an acknowledgment that the person who hurt you was raised in a broken world and most likely was abused, abandoned, or hurt in some way that led to his or her becoming an abuser. It is simply being aware of the reality that all life on earth is imperfect.

You live in such a life, and you live in it imperfectly. You, like everyone else, have done hurtful things to others. You are part of imperfect humanity. You share a bond of imperfection that comes out of God's gift of free choice. That gift has freed you to make up your own mind and choose your own priorities. By the exercise of that free will, you, like all of us, make poor choices and hurt others. And like most of us, you have been hurt by the poor choices of others.

This understanding is a key step toward gaining the new perspective you must have. When we have been abused or sinned against, we want to see ourselves as all good and our abuser as all bad. Seeing the other person in that way helps us survive the hurt. But changing our perspective leads us to see the truth—the other person is not all bad, and we are not all good. This true perspective enables us to move on and stop being victimized over and over again by our focus on a person who is no longer in our lives or an event we cannot change.

Both you and the person who hurt you make mistakes of your own free will. But it's likely that your abuser did not have a lot of support to make healthy choices. In this fallen world there are all kinds of influences to lead us off course—peer pressure, the media, poor parenting, not to mention a very real and alive Satan.

All of these influences have led to your being hurt. If you can see your hurt in a context of a world saturated with evil and see your abuser as having succumbed to those influences, it may lead you to a position where you gain the right perspective on him and the event that has blocked your life. This new perspective can lead you toward resolving your past and moving past your wall.

The Fourth Step toward a New Perspective

The fourth step toward gaining a truer perspective is a mind-set that provides you with a new way of looking at the past and those who hurt you. In addition, it will allow you to connect with those in the present who continue to inflict pain and stir up trouble in your life. It is simply having a forgiving spirit.

This forgiving spirit is a way of approaching all of life. It should not be confused with the actual act of forgiveness; it is rather a way to live with much less conflict and emotional turmoil. If you have ever seen someone in the midst of road rage, you know what it's like not to have this spirit. A person who stops a car to confront someone about his horrible driving is a person full of anger who lives on the edge of indicting everyone. That is a very hard life—as hard on the person living it as on the victims of his rage.

A forgiving mind-set enables you to avoid being eaten by this boiling cauldron of acid rage. You expect that people are going to slight you. You know that on any given day, you will have to forgive many slights, insults, and unintentional hurts. In this grace-filled way of life, you make a daily habit of ignoring the personal mistakes of others, and you make an effort to see every good thing that happens to you as a gift.

You say to yourself: "I can get over that." "I am going to let that go." "I can just turn that over and forget it." You develop an attitude of forgiveness and grace that makes you easy to live with. Better yet, it makes it easy for you to live inside your own skin.

This spirit of forgiveness allows you to stop personalizing everything unpleasant that happens to you and see the people behind the hurtful events. The poor service at the restaurant has nothing to do with you and a lot to do with the bad situation the server is experiencing at home. The guy who cuts you off in traffic may be late for his job for the last time before getting fired. His poor "traffetiquette" may have nothing to do with his wanting to hog the road or bulldoze you off it. Even if his aggressive driving is deliberate because he thinks he's superior to others on the road, he's still an object of pity for succumbing to whatever influences brought him to that unhappy delusion.

If you adopt this forgiving spirit, when the deeper hurts of life come along or linger, you tend to see them in a less personal way. You come to understand that you were abused because you were in the proximity of the person, not because you are a sitting duck for abuse or have been a target from the time you were born.

This mind-set gives you a reframed attitude that leads to a reframed life. You are more forgiving, less personalizing, and more others-centered.

Putting It All Together

To sum it up, what gets you unstuck from your past is a combination of humility, awareness, spiritual focus, and grace. These four components can completely change your outlook on anything from the past or in the present. They can help you get past your walls and move on toward a bright future.

In *humility,* you resist the temptation to see yourself as better than someone else. Jesus lived in humility. To walk as he did, you will sometimes need to take a step back and allow someone else to walk ahead. Your concern will be less for yourself and more for others.

In *awareness,* you realize we are all in this fallen world together, and you find ways to understand and connect, rather than declare a superior moral stance. You accept the imperfections of life rather than hold on to an ideal of perfection that neither you nor anyone else can attain. You understand your own imperfections as well as those of others.

With humility and awareness, you have a new *spiritual focus.* You live in the spiritual realm, tapping into a spiritual perspective that connects you to others who are drawn to you.

This spiritual focus gives you a spirit of forgiveness and new appreciation for *grace.* You understand that God gives you grace and loves you in spite of your imperfections. In gratitude for that gift, you gladly extend this grace to others, especially to those who have hurt you.

With this mind-set, you are able to get unstuck from the hurt of the past that has placed you behind a wall. Now you are ready to move on toward resolving your issue through grace.

When you take these four steps, you find yourself in a place where you can see even the vilest abuse from an altogether different and more accurate perspective. From this vantage point, you become open to resolving whatever has you stuck and putting it behind you. If you have been holding on to grudges, resentments, or bitterness for years, this new perspective allows you to let go of those pieces of contaminated plutonium and live your life in healthy freedom from the pain of the past. You can move into the future and live out the purposes God created you to accomplish.

You have achieved a resolution when some past event that was a dominating, negative influence in your life no longer has any power over you. The bad event no longer takes anything away from your life and, in fact, has added something to it. What you have learned from going through the reframing and resolving processes has made you an extremely strong person.

chapter eight

MOVING INTO THE FUTURE

Gaining a new and more accurate perspective on the hurts of the past is not an end in itself. It merely gets people unstuck from their pasts so they can take the healing step of resolving the difficulties that block their futures. The resolving step is difficult and often takes time, but it is where true healing takes place.

I do not believe in quick fixes and instant solutions. They produce nothing but false hopes and temporary results. They make you feel a little better for a while, but they soon drop you back into the place where you were before. It is like riding in a broken elevator. You push a button to get to the next floor. The bells and lights make you think you are ascending to a higher level. But when you open the door, you find you are on the same floor you thought you left. If you want to live your life above where you are now, you must be ready to strap yourself in and do the work required to get there. I can assure you that doing the hard work of resolving your issues is much easier than dealing with the consequences of failing to resolve them.

Sometimes the biggest culprit in undermining our attempts to resolve our issues is the all-you-have-to-do syndrome. It's natural to look for the easiest way out. Many overeaters remain overweight because of all-I-have-to-do thinking: "All I have to do is eat a salad at lunch. All I have to do is skip breakfast. All I have to do is eat slower." These are simplistic lies that fail to solve a very complex condition. When we abandon simplistic solutions and become willing to do whatever it takes, real change occurs.

Since losing weight is a huge wall in so many people's lives, let's stay with that example for a moment. In working with people who want to lose weight, I often see them turn to the quick fix of surgery, thinking "All I have to do" is have an operation, and the weight falls off and stays off. But it's only a matter of time before they are overweight again. It happens because they are looking for a solution that requires no personal responsibility—a solution that is done for them and excuses them from exercising the will and discipline required to achieve real results.

When people resort to surgery, they can succeed only if they are willing to follow the surgery by doing whatever it takes to become new people. The surgery gets the weight off, but it does not keep it off. Unless they make lifestyle changes, they will start adding fat and find themselves right back where they were before the surgery. Keeping weight off after surgery depends 100 percent on what they do. When people are willing and able to discipline themselves, there is a good chance the surgery will benefit them.

But if they are willing to make these changes on a regular basis, there is really little need to have the surgery. The point is, weight comes off when there is a willingness to do whatever it takes.

This principle applies to all our problems. Our problems get resolved when we develop a willingness to do whatever it takes. And what it takes is a willingness to reframe the past—to change our way of looking at past experiences that we have allowed to become walls. Whether it is the weight on our bodies or the weight of pain from past traumas or abuse, we can move past our walls and toward resolution only when we become willing to do *whatever it takes* to make it happen.

Resolving is the work that follows reframing. It is the next step past getting unstuck—the recovery of our lives.

THE ULTIMATE UPGRADE

I once went with my daughter's class on a field trip to Europe where her choir was competing. My worst nightmare is to be crammed into a tiny coach seat on a twelve-hour flight over the ocean. I get squeamish just thinking about it. But with all the courage I could muster, I boarded the plane and took my place in the little seat that made me feel very sorry for sardines. After hours of squirming, tossing, and twisting, it was with great relief that I walked off the plane in London.

On the day of our trip home, we returned to the airport, went through all the searches and security checks, and then sat in the waiting area for our flight. Above the rumble of chattering kids, I heard my name called. I walked to the desk and was handed a new boarding pass with a seat assignment in first class. My first thought was that someone must have sent the airline a movie of my writhing and moaning on the way over, and they were moved to pity. It was a mercy upgrade. But that was not the case. They simply had too many people show up for coach and used the alphabetical system to determine who got the upgrade. There are great advantages to having a name beginning with *A*. You cannot imagine how elated I felt to receive that upgrade.

In first class on Virgin Atlantic they give massages, serve gourmet food, and have seats that lie flat so you can sleep on little mattresses. This was luxury to the max, and it turned my trip home into a really great experience. That is what an upgrade can do.

What if you found that you could get an upgrade for your life? The good news is, you can! And the better news is that you don't have to wait for someone else to do it for you. You can upgrade your own life, leaving behind your misery or desperation.

You can upgrade the emotion of shame and replace it with acceptance and hope. You can upgrade from anger to understanding, forgiveness, love, and patience. You can upgrade from fear to confident peace. You can upgrade any emotion and live with a fresh state of mind if you are willing to do the work to earn the upgrade. I won't tell you that it's not hard work, but I can assure you it's always worth it.

UPGRADING FROM RESENTMENT TO LOVE

In the first chapter I briefly mentioned a man who decided to upgrade his life. With your indulgence, I will repeat that story here in order to make a different point. A very sick mother tragically abandoned this man as an infant. As he grew up, he felt entitled to hang on to the anger, bitterness, and sadness this produced. He had learned to survive, and he tried to convince himself he was getting along just fine. But he came to my workshop because he was filled with negativity and wanted to feel better.

Ironically, the day before the workshop began, his mother found him, made contact, and wanted to connect with him and become part of his life. Imagine how he must have felt. After a lifetime of not even knowing whether his mother was alive or dead, twenty years later, from out of nowhere, she shows up wanting to take her place as his mother and share his life.

All the anger, hurt, and bitterness this man had suppressed for so many years welled up within him. He wanted to hit her or at least shake her and tell her of all the misery he had endured because she had abandoned him. He rejected her offer to reconcile and demanded that she never contact him again.

On the first night of the workshop, he revealed this incident to the group. He shared his dismay and shock at the thought of this woman he had vilified all his life now wanting to be a happy family member. He could not imagine the possibility of any good in a woman who would forsake her infant child for twenty years with no contact or explanation. The group heard his description of his first brief meeting with this woman, and it was all bad. He broke down in tears as he finished.

On a hunch I asked him if he would be willing to do something. It would be difficult and painful, but it might lead to the beginning of a whole new life. He was willing. I told him that after the session was over, I wanted him to contact his birth mother and ask her about what happened in her childhood. I wanted him to discover the most hurtful thing she had been through and then report back to the group the next day. He promised to do it.

The next morning we saw a very different man come to the session. There was no look of rage on his face or sounds of fury from his mouth. He was calm and seemed to be at peace, but he had two of the most bloodshot eyes I have ever seen. I could not wait to find out what happened.

I called on him to tell the group what he had learned. Fighting back tears, he reported that he had called his mother and asked about her childhood. What he discovered changed his life forever. She told him she never knew her father, and her mother was regularly gripped by vast mood swings between deep depression and outbursts of rage. One day her mother took her next door to a neighbor's house and left her there. And her mother never came back.

The man's mother explained that this abandonment put her emotions out of control. So when he was born, she did to him exactly what her mother had done to her. She did it out of desperation, hoping he would never have to see her out of control—or worse, become the victim of her own angry attacks. She left him as an infant on her neighbors' doorstep, hoping they would give him a better life than she could. She told of praying for him every day and hoping that, unlike her own mother, she would someday be able to come back and be part of his life.

When he heard that, the young man immediately realized

that his mother was not evil. She simply acted according to what she had learned from her own mother. She had not specifically rejected him; she had rejected the concept of a child, not the person he would one day become. More precisely, in her mind it was an act of protection more than desertion, and her motive was for him to have a better life.

In the light of these new understandings, the young man began to reframe the entire incident, giving up resentment and anger and trading them for the beginnings of love. It was the start of his recovery from the deep wounds that had driven his life and controlled his destiny. With the new facts in hand, he reframed his mother, which unstuck him from his past. That step motivated him to resolve what he reframed and move past the unyielding wall he had bumped up against every day of his life. He was now free to move into a future of freedom.

THE PROCESS THAT LEADS TO RESOLUTION

I have written entire books on this process of resolution. *Healing Is a Choice* and *Transformation* give different perspectives on the process, and both can help you resolve what you have reframed. As we approach the end of this book, I want to present a list of resolution concepts that could help you move past the walls that block your future. I urge you to take these steps with someone who can guide and encourage you along the way.

1. *Examination.* Become a student of your own life. Take a look at the patterns you have developed. Plot the course you most often take when things become uncomfortable. Look for

the places where you hold the most negative emotions. What do you feel most often: anger? guilt? fear? What do you see as the cause of these emotions?

Start to look at yourself and your life objectively so you can develop a plan to resolve the areas of emotional contamination that keep you walled up in the darkness of the past.

2. *Openness and confession.* As our lives become focused on the horrible things others have done to us, we lose sight of our own shortcomings. Those we do see, we hide so no one will know just how sick or in need we are. We come to live in a cesspool of our own sins. In order to climb out of that, we need to risk becoming open about the struggles we are going through. We also need to confess the sins we are committing. We need to stop hiding and hunkering down and become willing to open up and confess. Openness gives an outlet to shame and stops its accumulation. Confession means we do not have to carry the shame with us.

3. *Focus on now.* Whatever happened in the past is over and finished. You cannot change it; you can only channel it. By channeling, I mean you take whatever pain you lived through and channel the power of it into something meaningful today. Today you are a survivor. Today you are living with many gifts, talents, and strengths. You must refuse to ruminate about the past that is over and wake up to the life you have now, focusing on the opportunities before you.

4. *Choosing to forgive.* I don't know of a tougher choice than the choice to forgive. But I don't know of another choice with as many rewards. There can be no resolution without forgiveness. We are commanded to forgive others as God has forgiven us. To

forgive only if we feel like it is not an option. We just have to do it. It may seem unfair to have to deal with the pain of what people have done to us and then go through the additional pain of forgiving them for doing it. They soil our slates with their misdeeds, and then we are asked to wipe their slates clean. This is so difficult that some people never do it.

I have often been confronted by victims of abuse who really believe they must not forgive. Some believe that if they forgive, they will seem to be giving the offender permission to do the same thing to them again. Some believe they don't have to forgive unless the other person repents. Some won't forgive unless forgiveness is specifically asked for.

But I believe that what the other person does is irrelevant. We need to forgive in order to free ourselves from bondage to the trauma the perpetrator inflicted. It won't come easily or instantly, but the sooner we begin, the sooner we can forgive and live free of the influence the evil has had on us.

The forgiveness process must also include us. We must offer ourselves the grace we give others and the grace God gives us. We must not beat ourselves up and shame ourselves over something we cannot change or undo. To resolve all the wounded areas of our lives, we must be willing to let go of the self-condemnation we have felt we deserved. Nothing is made better when we live hating ourselves for our mistakes. We must find a way to forgive the sins done to us and by us.

5. *Choosing to let go.* If there is anything more difficult than forgiving, it must be choosing to let go. Choosing to let go is the act of turning our lives and wills over to God. It is giving up the

control that makes us feel so important and keeps us distracted from doing the painful things that must be done to heal and transform our lives. Letting go is trusting God for the results. It is working, even though we may not yet see the end result of our work. It is a willingness to risk not having to be in charge of every moment of our lives.

For many of us who have been taught to take control, letting go is never easy. But it is one of the most powerful acts of faith. It is an open acknowledgment of our trust in God to take care of us. More than any other action, letting go and trusting God allows us to rest, be at peace, and know a life of serenity.

6. *Making amends and restitution.* Perhaps this is the most frequently neglected action in the process of resolving the issues that hold us back. When people have hurt us, we want them to pay a price. We don't want someone who has ruined our life to walk away scot-free. We want that person to pay for our suffering. We want to see a sacrifice that shows sincere remorse.

By the same token, others want the same from us. If we have betrayed them, we need to figure out what we can do to repair the damage. Of course nothing will totally make up for the evil we have done, but making amends, asking for forgiveness, saying "I'm sorry," paying back money taken, or replacing damaged goods can help us feel forgiven and live knowing that we did everything we could to make up for the loss and pain we caused.

7. *Making a plan to protect yourself.* Resolving your emotional traumas and conflicts can take a lot out of you. If you are not paying attention, you can easily fall back into your old ways. You

can build up the old resentments and repeat the old patterns that keep you stuck behind a wall.

When you protect yourself, you are less likely to have a relapse and get off the track toward purpose and meaning. You protect yourself by filling your life with healthy people. You find protection by being part of a small group, getting to know the members, and letting them know you.

Protection comes from always having a healthy place to go. It might be a therapist's office or a local codependency group meeting at Celebrate Recovery or Al-Anon.

Protection is a healthy sign of humility. It acknowledges that you are not brilliant enough to know when you may be vulnerable to relapse. You must have a plan to protect yourself from your past and from repeating the mistakes you have made.

8. *Fulfilling the dream of reaching others.* Those who are clinically obsessed find it hard to reach out authentically to others, because focus on *others* gets in the way of focus on *self.* When we focus heavily on self, it is easy to stumble from trauma into meaninglessness. Early on we need to begin reaching out to others. We need to secure our own progress by assisting others in their programs of healing. In this action we find meaning and purpose and a desire to go on living and contributing to a world that needs everyone's participation.

You can take these eight actions to resolve whatever has been troubling you. They are steps on an altogether different path from the ones most people choose to take. These steps will move you beyond just seeing things differently; they will move you beyond your walls and motivate you to live life to the fullest.

WHEN THE PAST OFFERS NO RESOLUTION

Perhaps you have been in a situation similar to the man left on the neighbors' front porch by his inadequate mother. But unlike his mother, yours did not come back to reveal the entire situation and provide you with resolution. Facts that will allow you to see your hurt in a new and different light are simply not available. You may think that since there is nothing new to be discovered, no emotional upgrade is available to you. You feel stuck and maybe a bit jealous of a man who had a parent care enough to come back. If that is your case, you still have reason to hope.

Let's say you have struggled your whole life with the pain of being sexually molested by a sick father who was an admired church leader. To everyone but you, he was known as a man of integrity who worked hard, provided for a family that looked perfect, attended church regularly, and taught Sunday school. Yet at night he would creep into your room, fondle you, tell you he loved you and that you were special. He would insist that you keep this little secret to yourself, or your mother would go crazy. She would hate you, and everything the family had would be lost. It was up to you to keep it all together. You had to endure the abuse and sacrifice yourself for the rest of the family. And just when you got old enough to want to do something about the past, he suddenly died, leaving you burdened with the terrible secret.

How can you resolve your pain? You will never hear an apology or confession or watch him be carried off to jail for the felony he committed against you. You will never get to tell him that for every moment of his sick pleasure, you have endured hours upon hours of anger, grief, horror, fear, and suicidal depression. You are left holding the bag you have been dragging around since the nightmare started.

How does someone in this situation upgrade to another level? How does someone struggling alone with this kind of secret find the way to get unstuck and move past the wall that now seems a permanent obstruction to a life of freedom? It is difficult but possible. You have to go back to the five walls and work through the ones that are blocking your life. Then, without a need for a response from anyone else, you must begin to work through the actions listed in this chapter that will lead you toward resolution.

When Is It Resolved?

If resolution is the goal, how do you know you have finally achieved it? You have achieved resolution when some past event that was a dominating, negative influence in your life no longer has any power over you. You remember what happened, but you don't relive the pain when you think back on it. The bad event no longer takes anything away from your life and, in fact, has added something to it. What you have learned from going through the perspective changes and resolving processes has made you an extremely strong person.

You know you have achieved resolution when you no longer hold a grudge against the person who hurt you. Instead, you have some degree of sympathy, or at least you pity him for the miserable life in which he is stuck. You now see the abuser's sickness for what it is, and you no longer resent him. You have risen above it, and you are free, because he no longer controls your life. You realize how much you have grown from working through all that happened to you, and you know you have reached the point where you will not repeat the trauma inflicted upon you. You are better, stronger, and wiser for what you have been through. You view it as something in your past, something you have conquered. It no longer poisons your present, and it certainly does not limit your future.

You have finally moved past the wall that has held you back for so long.

A wall confines you to a past that cannot be changed and to a future of more of the same. A boundary can open up the future, because it marks a change from the way things have gone in the past.

chapter**nine**

IS IT A
WALL OR
A BOUNDARY?

I find that there is often confusion about the difference between a wall and a boundary. Too often what people believe is a wall is actually a boundary, and what they believe is a boundary becomes a wall.

How do I distinguish between a wall I keep walking into and a boundary that allows me to walk in light and freedom? There are some vital distinctions, and below are some thoughts to help clarify the difference.

Case Study One

Lisa could have called her husband and told him this:

You may not come near me or phone me or contact me in any way. I don't want to see you, and I don't want to be part of your life. You're so messed up that you can't even see what you're doing to yourself, to me, and to the kids. So don't even think about coming back to me. It's not going to happen.

By making such a call, it might seem that Lisa would be setting a healthy boundary to protect her and her children from a husband who abused her in every way possible. But that is not the case. Instead, she would be building an indestructible wall that would keep her husband out forever.

After a few years of putting up with his sickness, Lisa finally faced the truth that he would not change. She became willing to do anything she needed to do to protect herself and her children from him. For a woman in her shoes, it would seem admirable for her to find the courage to impose a restraining order against her husband. But had she done that, she would have built a wall, rather than form a boundary.

A wall is all about what the *other person* needs to do and needs to stop. A boundary is all about what *I* am going to do and need to stop. If Lisa had set a healthy boundary, the call to her husband would have sounded more like this:

I've decided that I need to make some changes. I need to be separate from you for a while. If you can't honor that, then I will take our children and live in a safe place. I've decided that conversation with you is destructive, both to the children and to me. So until you've gotten help, I won't be taking phone calls from you or answering the door when you come to the house. I don't want to file a restraining order, but if that's what

I have to do, I will. When you're willing to get the help you need, I would love to talk with you about our kids and our future.

This is the course Lisa took, and her attitude, along with her suggestion of a possible restraining order, was a wake-up call to her husband. He immediately saw that the rules of the game had changed; he could no longer have his way with her. He had to make a couple of decisions: first, to stay away from her; and second, to get some help if there was to be any hope of the two of them getting back together again. That was something he wanted badly, now that he saw how easily he could lose her forever. He became willing to get the treatment that would tear down the walls that kept him trapped in anger and rage. And it was all because Lisa finally set a boundary.

CASE STUDY TWO

Janet told her husband that she would not be having sex with him until he went to a counselor and got help for all his problems that had surfaced in their one year of marriage. That sounds as if Janet was setting a healthy boundary. Nope. It was a wall that she built to avoid the vulnerability and intimacy required in making love with her husband.

The husband Janet had painted as all bad and loaded with problems certainly had some issues with which to deal. But he was not the real problem. She was. She was the one who needed to be seated in front of a counselor to work through her fear-plagued life that led her to want control of everything, especially her husband. She manipulated him and tried to control him by withdrawing from him sexually. She had constructed her wall so tall and wide and thick that it could never be torn down. But it was a wall her husband refused to walk into anymore, and he left her. She now had her wall, but she had no one to use it against. There was no one willing to be on the other side.

The Confinement of Walls and the Freedom of Boundaries

As these two case studies show, there is a big difference between a boundary and a wall. A wall confines you to a past that cannot be changed and to a future of more of the same. A boundary can open up the future, because it marks a change from the way things have gone in the past. Both provide some type of protection, but the protection of a wall limits all the positive outcomes, whereas the boundary has unlimited potential to secure a future of hope and healing.

On one hand, the wall means living as if the painful past must continue to be a present reality. It means living as if all the pain that was experienced as a five-year-old must still be experienced as a thirty-five-year-old. The wall gives no recognition of the fact that time has moved on. Strength has developed, and the things that were feared at five no longer have power at thirty-five, if one lives as an adult and not as a child.

Fear of all men at five might be helpful for survival to a girl who was abused at that age. But fear of all men at thirty-five is not helpful at all. It locks one inside the walls of the past, creating a self-imposed but needless prison, confining a person to attitudes and limitations that have no basis in reality and need not be perpetuated.

A boundary, on the other hand, is not a wall; it is a line in the sand, a line you draw around yourself that prevents the pain and suffering of the past from perpetuating itself. It is a stance that calls for action on your part if it is not honored. It is a statement of what I will do, what I have chosen, and what will be the outcome on my part, whether or not the other person gets the help or makes the changes needed.

Walls are used to make demands on the other person or nag him about the changes he must make. This approach merely causes the other person to build more defenses. A boundary works much more positively. It challenges the other person to drop the defenses and look at what needs to be changed.

I know I cannot change my past. I can only do what I can today to make way for a better future. Any focus I have on the past that causes me shame and distraction is going to hurt the future I am creating with my daily decisions. If I build a wall around my past, I am essentially protecting my past rather than me. A boundary does the opposite—it protects me today and leaves the past behind. That might mean I need to set a boundary that excludes someone who continues to bring up the past.

Walls are something you need to get past. You have to tear them down, go around them, or climb over them. They are to be overcome and shattered so you can move on. But boundaries are portable; you can take them with you. There is no time limit on a boundary, if I keep it in place. My first boundary is my skin—a boundary that comes with me, no matter what walls have been shattered or left behind. Like my skin, the boundary I set around myself becomes the moving protection for my life and future, rather than a wall that cuts me off from all options and keeps me needlessly confined to the traumas of the past.

It seems that walls are constructs of loneliness and isolation. They cut us off from building connection and community. But a boundary opens the doors to connection with healthy individuals in a healthy community. It helps us break out of isolation, because it creates a healthy barrier, insulating us from the unhealthy elements of life. A boundary leaves the sick stuff behind and opens us up to the healthy.

If I feel guilt, fear, or anger, there is a good chance I will build a wall to hide behind. The wall will prevent me from unleashing these emotions on others or prevent others from seeing them in me. If I can't resolve these issues, I am almost compelled to build a wall that hides either them or me or both.

Boundaries are not built on guilt, fear, or anger. They are built because a person has discovered and acted on the truth. Boundaries grow out of a new willingness to try something different that might move me out of guilt, fear, or anger. And boundaries require courage on my part. Brave people set up boundaries that lead them into new territory that is full of healthy options and meaningful relationships.

When I build a wall, it gives me a false sense of safety. I come to believe that, if my wall is strong enough, it will prevent me from being victimized again. But walls do not provide the safety one imagines. They can become so large that they crumble, allowing victimization to invade my life in other forms. Some people who think they are safely protected by their walls do not realize that their psyches have surreptitiously worked their way around the walls, exposing the very things they want to hide. Unlike a wall, a boundary actually brings authentic safety. It elicits the assistance of others when it is broken. It encourages connection to others. It provides the strength of safety in numbers, rather than the vulnerability of walled-off isolation.

When you hate yourself and fear the prospect of anyone finding out who you really are, you build a wall of defensiveness. But when you love yourself as a creature of God, you construct boundaries that honor the person you are and the God who created you. Boundaries are built on self-respect and good stewardship of all the gifts God has given you. The wall merely shuts out the light that reveals and nurtures those God-given gifts and strengths.

Finally and simply, a wall is a barrier. It is a barrier between others and the secrets I want to hide. It is a barrier that keeps me out and the sickness in. It is a barrier that prevents my seeing all the good I could have, keeps me focused on all the wrong that has hurt me, and sets me up to repeat those damaging experiences yet again.

The wall is a barrier, whereas a boundary is a beginning. It is the beginning of a life that does not allow evil to be inflicted on me. It is the beginning of searching for what is best and keeping out those influences that would prevent me from moving toward it. It is the beginning of a whole new way of being. It stops me from walking into walls and allows me to walk into the future with God and others in a healthy, life-giving community.

Do you want to stop walking into walls? Are you ready to knock them down once and for all? Then set some healthy boundaries—and keep them—for the sake of all that God has for you ahead.

STUDY GUIDE

Dear Friends,

This enhanced, interactive study guide has been prepared to help you get the most out of Walking into Walls. *It will enable you not only to review the insightful content from this book but to apply it more effectively to your life.*

At the beginning of each lesson, I've included a link where you can find a brief online video presentation of the material from me. It's a chance for us to talk heart-to-heart about that chapter's topic. You'll also find questions, exercises, and a Bible study to round out each lesson.

Most of the questions and exercises within this interactive guide are intended for personal study, but can easily be adapted for a group or class as well. Others are designed for group discussion or working through with a trusted confidant. (You'll find these clearly designated in each chapter.) The Bible study component of each lesson can be completed either on your own or in a group setting.

You will benefit most from this guide if you use the presentations, exercises, and questions in combination with each other. All together, these elements should assist you in crafting a plan that will enable you to enjoy life as God meant for you to enjoy it.

So now, if you're ready to stop crashing into walls and start walking into a new and blessed kind of life, let's get started!

STEVE ARTERBURN

Introduction
LEARNING TO SEE OUR WALLS

Before you begin, watch the "Learning to See Our Walls" online video presentation from Stephen Arterburn at worthypublishing .com/books/Walking-Into-Walls/.

The Main Point

Millions of people feel preoccupied with hurtful events and incidents that took place a long time ago in their past; and consequently, they allow erroneous beliefs to become barriers that keep them from a life of freedom, purpose, and meaning. Rather than resolve the pain and move on, they continue to bump against their walls, living as if a painful past were a present reality. But your story can be different!

Taking Stock

What erroneous beliefs or half-truths might be keeping you from seeing and acting on the truth? Take a look at the following statements, and after each one, circle the response that most closely reflects your own story.

- **This is not my fault.**

   Frequently say it   Occasionally say it   Seldom say it   Never say it

- **My parents just didn't get it.**

   Frequently say it   Occasionally say it   Seldom say it   Never say it

- **Nobody can help me but me.**

   Frequently say it   Occasionally say it   Seldom say it   Never say it

- **I know how to deal with this on my own.**

Frequently say it   Occasionally say it   Seldom say it   Never say it

- **I am not the one with the problem here.**

Frequently say it   Occasionally say it   Seldom say it   Never say it

- **How could this person hurt me, knowing how others have hurt me?**

Frequently say it   Occasionally say it   Seldom say it   Never say it

- **You have to be crazy to see a counselor.**

Frequently say it   Occasionally say it   Seldom say it   Never say it

- **Anyone would feel this way if he or she knew what I have been through.**

Frequently say it   Occasionally say it   Seldom say it   Never say it

- **When the person who hurt me makes a move toward resolution, I am prepared to respond, but not until then.**

Frequently say it   Occasionally say it   Seldom say it   Never say it

- **I'm so guilty that God can never forgive me.**

Frequently say it   Occasionally say it   Seldom say it   Never say it

Based on your responses to the preceding questions, what walls (if any) do you think may need your attention? Why?

_____

_____

_____

_____

Move Forward: For Personal Reflection

As you think about the invisible walls that may exist in your own life, ask yourself the following questions:

1. What walls of guilt, shame, anger, regret, or anxiety might be hurting me?

   _____

   _____

2. What erroneous beliefs might I hold, either about myself or about others (especially those who have hurt me)?

   _____

   _____

3. What do I see as my purpose in life?

   _____

   _____

4. How do I see my life in light of my past and current relationships?

   _____

   _____

5. What lies do the walls in my life represent? What truths do they hide?

   _____

   _____

Move Forward: For Discussion

1. What is "the mystery of misery"? Why is it important to understand?

2. Why is it necessary to deal with the walls in one's life?

3. How can you use the hurt in your past as a lens to observe your life?

4. How can friends and loved ones help us see and fulfill our life's purpose?

5. What does it mean to be free of a past that cannot be changed?

Listen for God's Voice

Saul, the first king of Israel, ultimately failed in his role as ruler, largely because he kept crashing into the wall of fear and never learned to move beyond it.

Read 1 Samuel 10:22; 15:24; 18:12, 15, 29; 28:5.

1. What do all of these texts have in common?

2. How did Saul respond to the wall of fear? What do you think he was afraid of?

3. What kind of legacy did Saul leave behind?

4. How might Saul's story have turned out differently? What choices could have helped him?

Read 2 Timothy 1:7.

1. What did God *not* give to us?

2. What *did* God give to us?

3. How can the message of this verse help believers to destroy the wall of fear?

4. How might you need to integrate the truth of this verse in your own life?

What You Can Do Now

After reading the introduction, pondering its message on your own, discussing its ideas with others, and working through the preceding exercises and questions, *what do you need to do now?* Use the space below to outline a plan of attack to identify and move beyond the walls that are keeping you from enjoying the blessed future God has for you.

_____

_____

_____

_____

1

PHANTOM WALLS THAT STOP US

Before you begin, watch the "Phantom Walls That Stop Us" online video presentation from Stephen Arterburn at worthypublishing .com/books/Walking-Into-Walls/.

The Main Point

The walls that keep us from experiencing joy and health—walls such as anger, resentment, and guilt—are often built out of incomplete or misunderstood pieces of reality, and from half-truths that prevent us from perceiving the real truth. We focus so resolutely on an ugly pebble that we miss the majestic mountain on which it rests. Don't let that pebble keep you from enjoying the majestic view!

Taking Stock

Do you find yourself often mulling over some painful event from your past, even your distant past? If so, what does that mental conversation look like? Who is the hero? Who is the villain? Who is the victim? What happened? What was the result? With that hurtful incident in mind, respond to the following statements.

- **I know all I need to know about the one who hurt me.**
  True/False

- **My current problems are the perpetrator's fault.**
  True/False

- **The one who hurt me is pure evil.**
  True/False

- **I consider myself a victim.**
  True/False

- **I am the innocent target of undeserved abuse.**
  True/False

- **This one horrible event ruined my life forever.**
  True/False

Based on your responses to the preceding questions, do you believe you might have some phantom walls that need to come down in order for you to move ahead? If so, what might they be? What can you do about them?

_____

_____

_____

_____

Move Forward: For Personal Reflection

Phantom walls create barriers of anger, resentment, and guilt. They also prompt you to view your strengths as weaknesses, to exaggerate the deficits in your life, and to crowd out any sense that God made you to be a capable person.

1. Do you ever play the victim? Explain.

   _____

   _____

2. Is there some event or incident from your past that tends to act as the framework from which you interpret life? If so, describe it.

   _____

   _____

3. What do you know about the personal history of the person who has hurt you deeply?

_____

_____

4. What false conclusions do you think you might have come to in regard to yourself and your life?

_____

_____

5. What aspect of Jesus' truth do you think he most wants you to grasp?

_____

_____

Move Forward: For Discussion

1. How can half-truths cloud one's perception of the full truth? Give some examples.

2. How is it possible to look at life from a broader perspective than the one you currently may have? How do we expand our perspective?

3. What does it mean to "personalize the hurt" when thinking about some painful incident from the past? How can this, in itself, cause further hurt?

4. What does it mean to take responsibility for your life in the area of your emotions? How can this be done?

5. How might God use your common experience of pain or "bonds of neglect" to heal you and help others?

Listen for God's Voice

Read Matthew 16:5-12.

1. What did the disciples not understand? What kept them from understanding?

2. To what false conclusion did their failure to understand lead them?

3. How did Jesus correct their misunderstanding?

4. In what way did the disciples' failure to understand become a wall that kept them from experiencing all that God had for them?

5. Why do you think Jesus made his disciples work to correct their misunderstanding? Why didn't he just explain their error and then provide the right answer? What does this suggest for how God will work in your own life?

Read Luke 24:13-32.

1. What incomplete or misunderstood pieces of information caused problems for the two disciples described in this passage?

2. How did Jesus deal with this misunderstanding? What actions did he take to dismantle the wall?

3. How did this incomplete understanding affect the emotions of the two disciples?

4. What happened once the wall came down? How did the emotions of the disciples change?

5. What does this incident suggest to you about the way God tends to deal with the walls in your own life?

What You Can Do Now

After reading chapter 1, pondering its message on your own, discussing its ideas with others, and working through the preceding exercises and questions, *what do you need to do now?* Use the space below to outline a plan of attack to move beyond your phantom walls and toward the blessed future God has for you.

_____

_____

_____

2
THE WALL OF STUBBORN RESISTANCE

Before you begin, watch "The Wall of Stubborn Resistance" online video presentation from Stephen Arterburn at worthypublishing .com/books/Walking-Into-Walls/.

The Main Point

Stubborn resistance is an unhelpful, contrarian attitude that leads people to think, *Since I already know everything there is to know on this topic, no one can help me.* Stubborn resistance keeps people stuck in their problems and keeps them from seeing their blind spots—and so they continue to walk into walls they can't see, and so they continue to hurt themselves. Here's help for getting out of the rut and getting on with your life.

Taking Stock

Read the following statements and respond with the answer that most closely matches your own situation. How stubbornly resistant do your answers suggest you might be?

- **I frequently admit I am wrong.**
  True/False

- **I frequently ask people for their opinion.**
  True/False

- **I often admit that I have approached problems in unhealthy ways.**
  True/False

- **I willingly admit that I may need help to move beyond the walls in my life.**
  True/False

- **I have said to my spouse, "You knew I was this way when you married me."**
  True/False

- **I tend to be a "my way or the highway" kind of person.**
  True/False

- **People have told me (or I feel) that I have a strong need always to be right.**
  True/False

- **I stop listening to people who try to get me to see things in different ways.**
  True/False

Based on your answers to these questions, what might you have to do in order to become more open-minded to listening to outside perspectives? List some possible actions below.

_____

_____

_____

Move Forward: For Personal Reflection

Several key things must happen in order for someone to escape the grip of stubborn resistance and move forward into God's best. This section asks you to look deeper into your own experience and explore what you might need to do in order to get unstuck.

Become more self-aware.

1. What do you see as your most difficult problem?

2. What blind spots have others tried to discuss with you in this area of your life?

3. What walls do you keep running into that stop your forward progress?

4. Might there be a deeper reality that lies behind your problem? What guilt or shame might you be carrying regarding some deeply painful event in your past? What is the "it" that keeps you from moving forward?

5. How could your parents or grandparents have contributed to the problem you now face?

Look honestly at yourself.

1. What walls in your life have you refused to recognize?

2. How have you defended and rationalized your behavior?

3. In what ways have you tried to project your own problem on to others?

4. How do you normally react to those who challenge you regarding this problem?

5. How might the loss of your walls make you afraid? How have these walls brought you comfort in the past? How do these walls help you avoid the pain of self-examination?

Move Forward: For Discussion

Seek the wisdom of others.

1. How have others dealt successfully with the wall that confronts you?

2. How have others overcome the guilt or shame that once kept them stuck?

3. What counsel might others offer to help you get beyond your fear?

Advance to willingness.

To move forward into God's best for you, you must be willing to overcome any stubborn resistance that you discover in yourself. Discuss the following questions to gauge that willingness, and to discover how to experience God's best.

1. To whom do you need to listen more carefully in order to overcome the wall of stubborn resistance in your life?

2. What plan do you have to accomplish your dreams? Describe it.

3. What are you willing to do to improve your life? Be specific.

4. What work must you do to replace stubborn resistance with an open-minded willingness to look objectively at your life, listen to the wisdom of others, and move toward real change?

Make yourself accountable to others who care about you.

1. Who are the safe truth-tellers in your life?

2. Who specifically might make a good accountability partner for you?

Listen for God's Voice

The book of Jeremiah speaks more about the dangers of stubborn resistance than perhaps any other book in the Bible. Jeremiah warned his people repeatedly that if they did not turn from their stubbornness, change their ways, and begin to look at life from God's perspective, they would face hardship, pain, and even tragedy. Yet if they would listen, a world of great possibilities would open to them.

Read Jeremiah 7:23-24.

1. What kept the people from moving forward? Why did they go backward?

2. What was the result of this failure?

3. What is God's desire for all his people? (v. 23)

4. What is required to stop following the stubborn inclinations of an evil heart? What does it mean to "listen" and "pay attention" (v. 24 NIV)? What do those actions require?

Read Jeremiah 18:11-17.

1. What does the command to "turn" (NIV) involve?

2. What does the command to "reform" (NIV) involve?

3. What consequences come with a commitment to stubborn resistance?

Read Exodus 5:1-14:31.

The Pharaoh of the biblical exodus is perhaps the best illustration in Scripture of someone who hardened his heart and refused to listen to outside perspectives. Through his stubborn resistance, he caused not only his own destruction but also the ruin of his people.

Compare two sets of verses about this incident:
Read Exodus 7:13, 22; 8:15, 19, 32.
Read Exodus 9:12, 34; 10:1, 20, 27; 11:10; 14:8.

1. What is similar about these two sets of verses?

2. What is different about these two sets of verses?

3. What do you conclude about someone who repeatedly hardens his or her heart against God's best?

Stubborn resistance was a problem in the New Testament era as well as in Old Testament days. Read the following verses, recount the issues described in each passage, and then suggest how the issues back then continue to pose a problem for us today.
Read Mark 3:1-6; 16:14.
Read Romans 2:1-5.

What You Can Do Now

After reading chapter 2, pondering its message on your own, discussing its ideas with others, and working through the preceding exercises and questions, *what do you need to do now?* Use the space below to outline a plan of attack to move beyond the wall of stubborn resistance and toward the blessed future God has for you.

_____

_____

_____

_____

3
THE WALL OF ARROGANT ENTITLEMENT

*Before you begin, watch "The Wall of Arrogant Entitlement" online
video presentation from Stephen Arterburn at worthypublishing
.com/books/Walking-Into-Walls/.*

The Main Point

The wall of arrogant entitlement grows out of an adolescent
state of mind that sees itself as the center of the universe. Those
afflicted with it believe they have a right to be happy at all costs,
and so they rationalize selfish and destructive behaviors in order
to get what they think they deserve. The predictable result is
pain, both for them and for others. Thankfully, maturity—and
a positive, purposeful life—await those who will persist in getting past "my way" thinking.

Taking Stock

People trapped by the wall of arrogant entitlement often not only
rationalize their behavior but speak it out loud. They justify their
actions with comments such as those below. How often do you
find yourself saying . . .

- **I deserve this.**

  Frequently say it   Occasionally say it   Seldom say it   Never say it

- **I have real needs that are not getting met.**

  Frequently say it   Occasionally say it   Seldom say it   Never say it

- **I am in a crisis, and this one thing will ease it.**

  Frequently say it   Occasionally say it   Seldom say it   Never say it

- **This really isn't betrayal; and besides, he/she won't ever know.**

  Frequently say it   Occasionally say it   Seldom say it   Never say it

- **This person really disappointed me. So it's actually his/her fault.**

  Frequently say it   Occasionally say it   Seldom say it   Never say it

- **Anyone in my situation would do the same thing.**

  Frequently say it   Occasionally say it   Seldom say it   Never say it

- **I'm not fully responsible for my actions, because I'm an addict.**

  Frequently say it   Occasionally say it   Seldom say it   Never say it

If you say these things to yourself enough, you will eventually build a bridge that enables you to cross over into arrogant entitlement. You will rationalize your actions in a way that makes the wrong seem quite acceptable, "given the circumstances." What do your responses to the preceding questions indicate to you? What action, if any, do they suggest you need to take?

_____

_____

_____

_____

Move Forward: For Personal Reflection

1. Do you find yourself talking and thinking more about "rights" or about "responsibilities"? Explain.

   _____

   _____

2. What things have you done to achieve so-called happiness that actually led to grief? Why do you think this happened?

   _____

   _____

3. In what ways are you actively involved in helping others?

   _____

   _____

4. What are you doing to improve your relationship with God?

   _____

   _____

5. In what areas of your life are you content? In what areas do you lack contentment? Explain.

   _____

   _____

Move Forward: For Discussion

1. What other songs besides "My Way" can you think of that reflect an attitude of entitlement?

2. Describe some rationalizations you have heard from individuals who tried to explain why their "right" to happiness led to questionable behavior.

3. Why and how does arrogant entitlement tend to destroy relationships?

4. How would you describe humility? Why is it the key to overcoming the wall of arrogant entitlement?

5. What does it mean to surrender everything to God? How is this done?

Listen for God's Voice

Read Philippians 2:3-11.

1. What personal quality or trait is highlighted in this passage?

2. How does Jesus exemplify this quality or trait?

3. How should this quality affect the way we treat others?

4. How does this quality help to break down the wall of arrogant entitlement?

5. How are we to nurture this quality in ourselves? How can we make it grow?

Read 1 Peter 5:5-7.

1. What does it mean to submit to one another? What does this look like in practice?

2. How do you "clothe yourself" (NIV) with humility? What is significant about the metaphor of putting on humility like a change of wardrobe?

3. What reason does Peter give for humbling ourselves in verse 6?

4. What is the connection between the promise of verse 6 and the statement of verse 7? How does verse 7 make it easier for us to count on the promise of verse 6?

5. Who is the most humble person you know? How do others react to him or her? How can humility improve your own life?

What You Can Do Now

After reading chapter 3, pondering its message on your own, discussing its ideas with others, and working through the preceding exercises and questions, *what do you need to do now?* Use the space below to outline a plan of attack to move beyond the wall of arrogant entitlement and toward the blessed future God has for you.

_____

_____

_____

_____

_____

_____

4
THE WALL OF JUSTIFIABLE RESENTMENT

Before you begin, watch "The Wall of Justifiable Resentment" online video presentation from Stephen Arterburn at worthypublishing .com/books/Walking-Into-Walls/.

The Main Point

Many people languish behind a wall of justifiable resentment, remaining angry and bitter over some injustice done to them. They stew over the hurt and dream of ways to force the perpetrator to make things right (or at least to suffer for the wrong committed), even as they live in a self-imposed prison that blocks off their future. But you can find release from resentment and breathe the fresh air of freedom if you'll work through your experiences and emotions, step by step.

Taking Stock

Unresolved bitterness and resentment can eat you up inside and leave you chained to a hurtful past—long after the one who hurt you has forgotten about the whole painful affair. Read the following statements and, after each one, circle the answer that best represents your perspective.

- **Forgiving that person would be tantamount to letting him/her off the hook.**

Strongly agree   Moderately agree   Moderately disagree   Totally disagree

- **I have every right to be angry about what he/she did to me.**

Strongly agree   Moderately agree   Moderately disagree   Totally disagree

- **I fantasize about bad things happening to the perpetrator.**

Strongly agree   Moderately agree   Moderately disagree   Totally disagree

- **He/she is to blame for my crummy life.**

Strongly agree   Moderately agree   Moderately disagree   Totally disagree

- **I often tell others what this person did to me.**

Strongly agree   Moderately agree   Moderately disagree   Totally disagree

- **I seem to be angry a lot of the time.**

Strongly agree   Moderately agree   Moderately disagree   Totally disagree

Based on your answers to the preceding questions, what do you think you may need to do in order to avoid the wall of justifiable resentment?

_____

_____

_____

_____

Move Forward: For Personal Reflection

Human beings were not designed to live with resentment, justifiable or otherwise. Bitterness in the heart works like a corrosive on the soul, eating away at our insides and poisoning everything.

It also makes little practical sense, since in harboring a grudge, we chain ourselves to the very person who hurt us.

1. How do you normally react when someone does something to hurt you? Do you easily forgive, or do you tend to hold on to the slight and keep replaying what happened? Explain.

   _____

   _____

2. How easy would it be for you to put yourself in the offender's shoes for a time? Explain.

   _____

   _____

3. Think of the worst thing anyone ever did to you. Have you forgiven this person? Explain.

   _____

   _____

4. What would it mean for you to focus on your response, rather than on the actions of the one who hurt you?

   _____

   _____

Move Forward: For Discussion

1. What does it mean to "humanize" the offender, and why is this important?

2. How can people work through their fear of the future,

especially a fear caused by the worry that someone will hurt them again? What are some good strategies?

3. What are some proven ways to help others who are hurting? What have you seen that works?

4. In what way is forgiveness a process, and not merely a one-time event? Describe what this process might look like.

5. How can a person know they have truly forgiven their offender?

Listen for God's Voice

The Bible has a lot to say about the necessity of forgiveness and the devastation caused by unresolved bitterness, long-held resentment, and smoldering anger. God designed forgiveness not only to cleanse us spiritually but to make us whole emotionally and physically. Consider just four of the Bible's many passages on this issue.

Read Matthew 6:14-15.

1. What does this passage tell us about the importance of forgiving those who injure us?

2. What does an unwillingness to forgive reveal about our hearts?

Read Ephesians 4:31-32 and Colossians 3:13.

1. What command are we given in verse 31? How comprehensive is this command?

2. How is it possible to obey the command of verse 32? What outside help do we need?

3. Why are we to forgive, according to verse 32 and Colossians 3:13?

Read Hebrews 12:14-15.

1. How are the pursuit of peace and the pursuit of holiness related? What connects them?

2. What does a root of bitterness have to do with falling short of the grace of God? How does bitterness cause trouble and defile people?

What You Can Do Now

After reading chapter 4, pondering its message on your own, discussing its ideas with others, and working through the preceding exercises and questions, *what do you need to do now?* Use the space below to outline a plan of attack to move beyond the wall of justifiable resentment and toward the blessed future God has for you.

_____

_____

_____

_____

_____

_____

5
THE WALL OF DISCONNECTED ISOLATION

Before you begin, watch "The Wall of Disconnected Isolation" online video presentation from Stephen Arterburn at worthypublishing.com/books/Walking-Into-Walls/.

The Main Point

We have been created to develop strong relationships with other people and with God, but painful experiences can prompt some of us to isolate ourselves in the vain hope of escaping further pain. What's wrong with that? In isolation, a person will have a much tougher time knowing who they are. They're also prone to remain ignorant of their need for growth in many key areas of life—and this leads to greater pain, not less. Don't isolate yourself. Strive to develop and build relationships that will give your life meaning and purpose.

Taking Stock

How connected are you with others? How deeply do others know you? Respond to each of the statements below with the answer that best corresponds to the way you think, feel, and operate.

- **I'm just fine the way I am—God is all I need.**

Strongly agree   Moderately agree   Moderately disagree   Totally disagree

- **I really don't like being around people who are in pain.**

Strongly agree   Moderately agree   Moderately disagree   Totally disagree

- **I have too many of my own needs to be of much help to others in need.**

Strongly agree   Moderately agree   Moderately disagree   Totally disagree

- **I'm known as an especially empathetic person.**

Strongly agree   Moderately agree   Moderately disagree   Totally disagree

- **I'm well acquainted with the areas in which I most need personal growth.**

Strongly agree   Moderately agree   Moderately disagree   Totally disagree

- **Others tend to see me as a needy person.**

Strongly agree   Moderately agree   Moderately disagree   Totally disagree

Based on the answers you've just given, what might you need to do to overcome the wall of disconnected isolation?

_____

_____

_____

_____

Move Forward: For Personal Reflection

1. In the space below, write down the three areas in which you think you see the greatest need for your own spiritual or emotional growth.

   _____

   _____

2. Think back on the most personal conversations you've had over the past month. What do you think others would say are the areas of growth that you most need to address?

   _____

   _____

3. How easy is it for you to empathize with the pain of someone else? Explain.

   _____

   _____

4. Among your friends and close associates, who are the most objective and insightful observers you know who could speak truth into your life? List them.

   _____

   _____

5. This week, how can you practice being more vulnerable with the people who are closest to you?

   _____

   _____

Move Forward: For Discussion

1. Why do we need others to help us see who we really are and the areas of our lives that need the most attention?

2. Name some helpful and affirming ways that we can encourage our loved ones to do some honest self-evaluation.

3. How does relational intimacy (as opposed to merely sex-

ual intimacy) lead to joy, fulfillment, and a broadened perspective?

4. Name some effective strategies for getting to know people for who they really are, warts and all.

5. What does mutual submission look like in the body of Christ?

Listen for God's Voice

The New Testament is famous for its "one another" passages, all of which emphasize the necessity of connecting at deep levels with other believers in Christ. Look up a few of these passages, and discuss why interconnectedness is so important in God's kingdom.

Read John 17:10-11, 20-24.

1. What kind of intimacy did Jesus pray for in this passage? How much of this intimacy have you experienced? Explain.

2. What did Jesus mean when he prayed that his followers would be "one as we are one" (v. 11 NIV)?

3. Why does Jesus pray that his followers may be "one"? What does such unity communicate to the outside world? Why is that important?

Read Romans 14:19.

1. What kind of things tend to lead to peace? Are you pursuing them? Explain.

2. What kind of things edify, or build up, other believers? What are you doing to build up other believers? Are you doing anything that might tend to tear them down? If so, how can you turn things around?

What You Can Do Now

After reading chapter 5, pondering its message on your own, discussing its ideas with others, and working through the preceding exercises and questions, *what do you need to do now?* Use the space below to outline a plan of attack to move beyond the wall of disconnected isolation and toward the blessed future God has for you.

_____

_____

_____

_____

6
THE WALL OF BLIND IGNORANCE

Before you begin, watch "The Wall of Blind Ignorance" online video presentation from Stephen Arterburn at worthypublishing.com/ books/Walking-Into-Walls/.

The Main Point

All of us have blind spots that, if left unattended, will cause us great pain and make satisfying relationships difficult, if not impossible. To see our lives and ourselves from another's perspective can make all the difference between frustration and fulfillment. Don't be afraid to seek out the mirrors God has provided to help you get on with your life. His truth, in combination with the feedback of other people, can transform your life!

Taking Stock

Given our blind spots, we require outside perspectives to help us see the truth. How open are you to those outside perspectives? Circle the answer to each of the following statements that you believe most accurately reflects your situation.

- **I am quite good at seeing my life from the perspective of others.**

  Strongly agree   Moderately agree   Moderately disagree   Totally disagree

- **I see the faults of others much more readily than I see my own faults.**

  Strongly agree   Moderately agree   Moderately disagree   Totally disagree

- **I often invite others to speak truth into my life.**

  Strongly agree   Moderately agree   Moderately disagree   Totally disagree

- **I am very good at applying God's truth to my life, even in difficult areas.**

  Strongly agree   Moderately agree   Moderately disagree   Totally disagree

- **I can easily name my top three blind spots.**

  Strongly agree   Moderately agree   Moderately disagree   Totally disagree

- **I am totally committed to obeying whatever God might command me to do.**

Strongly agree Moderately agree Moderately disagree Totally disagree

Based on the answers you've just given, what might you need to do to overcome the wall of blind ignorance?

_____

_____

_____

Move Forward: For Personal Reflection

We are all ignorant about some things, but when we remain willfully ignorant about things we should know, that's when problems arise. Though God calls us to take off the blinders, we feel a certain comfort in remaining in the dark, especially when stepping into the light would require us to make some changes in how we live. To make those changes, we need to be open to the truth God reveals to us so we can become aware of our blind spots and learn to *see*.

1. Describe the last time you became aware of a blind spot in your life. What happened?

   _____

   _____

2. What "log" might Jesus be telling you to take out of your own eye before you criticize the speck in someone else's eye?

   _____

   _____

3. What are some of the lies that you tend to tell yourself?

_____

_____

4. What biblical commands are the hardest for you to heed? Why?

_____

_____

Move Forward: For Discussion

1. How has seeing things from another's perspective brought healing to your friends and loved ones?

2. In what ways can probing beneath the surface be helpful?

3. How can you best encourage one another to obey the Lord, even when it seems difficult to do so?

4. Not everyone effectively speaks truth into the lives of others. How have you seen this done well . . . and not so well?

5. Why is obedience the key to overcoming blind ignorance? Why does one have to obey the truth in order to know it?

Listen for God's Voice

Read Matthew 7:3-5.

1. Why does Jesus ask the question in verse 3?

2. Why does Jesus repeat the question in another form in verse 4?

3. What counsel does Jesus give in verse 5?

4. What would "removing the log" look like in your life?

Read John 7:17; 8:31-32.

1. What promise does Jesus give in John 7:17? What practical implications does this suggest to you?

2. What does it mean to abide in Jesus' word (8:31)?

3. How can we know the truth? How does this truth set us free? Free from what?

What You Can Do Now

After reading chapter 6, pondering its message on your own, discussing its ideas with others, and working through the preceding exercises and questions, *what do you need to do now?* Use the space below to outline a plan of attack to move beyond the wall of blind ignorance and toward the blessed future God has for you.

_____

_____

_____

_____

_____

_____

_____

_____

7
GETTING UNSTUCK

Before you begin, watch the "Getting Unstuck" online video presentation from Stephen Arterburn at worthypublishing.com/books/ Walking-Into-Walls/.

The Main Point

Many people remain stuck behind hurtful walls because they fear what might happen if they break through those walls; they fear that they might have to take risks, or take responsibility for their painful situations, or engage fully in life. Yet by changing how they think about their past, they find a key to the door of a great new future. Take a chance on yourself, your future, and God today. Reach out—and open the door. You are not alone!

Taking Stock

When you remain stuck behind walls, you hold on to thoughts and feelings that distort your outlook and damage your health. Consider several examples of inaccurate thinking about yourself and others, and circle the response after each that most closely reflects your situation.

- **I have a crummy set of genes, and therefore I am always going to be sick, just as my parents were.**

  Strongly agree   Moderately agree   Moderately disagree   Totally disagree

- **I have always been a bit down at every stage of my life.**

  Strongly agree   Moderately agree   Moderately disagree   Totally disagree

- **My loneliness keeps me locked up and in bed a lot.**

Strongly agree   Moderately agree   Moderately disagree   Totally disagree

- **It's just my lot in life to feel miserable.**

Strongly agree   Moderately agree   Moderately disagree   Totally disagree

- **The person who hurt me is all bad.**

Strongly agree   Moderately agree   Moderately disagree   Totally disagree

- **The perpetrator has no regrets.**

Strongly agree   Moderately agree   Moderately disagree   Totally disagree

- **The offender is beyond redemption.**

Strongly agree   Moderately agree   Moderately disagree   Totally disagree

- **That person deserves nothing good.**

Strongly agree   Moderately agree   Moderately disagree   Totally disagree

- **That person has nothing of value to offer this world.**

Strongly agree   Moderately agree   Moderately disagree   Totally disagree

Based on your responses to the preceding questions, what might you have to do adjust the way you think about either yourself or others?

_____

_____

_____

_____

Move Forward: For Personal Reflection

1. Think about situations in your past when you refused to make some needed changes because you saw benefit to living in the old way. What "benefits" were you reluctant to give up? In the end, how beneficial to you were these "benefits"?

   _____

   _____

2. Describe how it might truly benefit you to start thinking differently about your past.

   _____

   _____

3. Think about the person who hurt you. What kind of broken past does he/she also have?

   _____

   _____

4. What new "frame" or perspective might help you to see yourself in a more accurate, biblical light?

   _____

   _____

5. What new "frame" or perspective might help you to see the perpetrator in a more accurate, biblical light?

   _____

   _____

Move Forward: For Discussion

1. How does acknowledging our sin (Romans 3:23) take away any morally superior ground we might have thought we owned?

2. How are we able to access the Holy Spirit's power for whatever challenge we face?

3. How can we develop a forgiving spirit or mind-set, as opposed to merely granting instances of forgiveness? Why should a forgiving attitude be our goal?

4. How is accessing God's grace a key to getting unstuck? What does it mean, in a practical sense, to access God's grace?

5. Have each person share some instances when they managed to get unstuck. What did they do to get unstuck? What happened as a result of getting unstuck?

Listen for God's Voice

Read Ephesians 2:10-18.

1. List all the truths about yourself that this passage teaches.

2. List all the benefits of belonging to Christ that this passage teaches.

3. Explain how this passage describes your former life, outside of Christ.

4. What difference does it make to you, on a day-to-day basis, that you are now "in Christ" (NIV)? How does this knowledge shape your daily experience?

Read Galatians 5:16-25.

1. What does it mean to "walk in the Spirit" (NIV)? How is this accomplished?

2. What is the result of not walking in the Spirit? (see vv. 19-21)

3. What is the result of walking in the Spirit? (see vv. 22-24)

4. What is the difference between "living" in the Spirit and "walking" in the Spirit? How are they related?

What You Can Do Now

After reading chapter 7, pondering its message on your own, discussing its ideas with others, and working through the preceding exercises and questions, *what do you need to do now?* Use the space below to outline a plan of attack to get unstuck and move toward the blessed future God has for you.

_____

_____

_____

_____

_____

8
MOVING INTO THE FUTURE

Before you begin, watch the "Moving into the Future" online video presentation from Stephen Arterburn at worthypublishing.com/ books/Walking-Into-Walls/.

The Main Point

While it takes hard work to build a fulfilling present out of the embers of a painful past—and there are no easy answers or short-cuts to gaining a more fulfilling life—those who want to move forward will do whatever it takes to grasp God's best for them. And by making such a commitment to upgrading their life, they exchange fear for a confident peace. That peace and confidence is yours for the taking. Pursue that "better life" that God has for you with all your heart, mind, and strength!

Taking Stock

Walls don't dissolve or disappear on their own; resolving the painful issues of your past requires a firm commitment from you to bring down those walls. To see how ready you might be for this step of resolution, respond to each of the following statements with the answer that best reflects your current situation.

- **I am ready for the hard work it takes to build a new and better life.**

  Strongly agree Moderately agree Moderately disagree Totally disagree

- I often tell myself, "All I have to do is _____"
to solve my problems.

Strongly agree Moderately agree   Moderately disagree   Totally disagree

- I have a "whatever it takes" approach to moving on to a future of freedom.

Strongly agree Moderately agree   Moderately disagree   Totally disagree

- I feel as though I am stuck in the past and can't move forward.

Strongly agree Moderately agree   Moderately disagree   Totally disagree

- I have turned my life and my will over to God, trusting him for the outcome.

Strongly agree Moderately agree   Moderately disagree   Totally disagree

- I believe my painful past can actually assist me in building a bright future.

Strongly agree Moderately agree   Moderately disagree   Totally disagree

As you consider your preceding answers, what might you need to do now in order to resolve your issues with painful events from your past and get ready to move into a brighter future?

_____

_____

_____

_____

_____

Move Forward: For Personal Reflection

1. In what areas of your life do you think you most need to move forward?

    _____

    _____

2. What fears in your life most need to be replaced with a confident peace?

    _____

    _____

3. What sinful patterns do you need to acknowledge, confess, and forsake?

    _____

    _____

4. With whom do you need to make amends? What kind of restitution may be necessary?

    _____

    _____

5. Outline your plan to protect yourself in the future.

    _____

    _____

Move Forward: For Discussion

1. What does it mean to "reframe your past" in order to move forward?

2. In what way(s) would you like to upgrade your life? Dream a little together.

3. How can you encourage each other to focus on *now* rather than on *then?*

4. It's usually easier to reach out to others when you're with a supportive group. How can you come together to reach out?

5. How can you effectively remind each other that your past doesn't have to keep taking from you, but instead can add something valuable to your life?

Listen for God's Voice

Read Deuteronomy 30:19-20.

1. What would a choice for "life" (NIV) look like for you? How would it benefit you?

2. What would a choice for "death" (NIV) look like for you? How would it hurt you?

3. How can the choices you make now affect your children and your descendants?

Read Galatians 4:28-5:1.

1. What does it mean to be a "child of promise" (NIV)?

2. What does it mean to be free in Christ?

3. How can you stand firm in your liberty in Christ? How can you avoid getting entangled in bondage or slavery?

What You Can Do Now

After reading chapter 8, pondering its message on your own, discussing its ideas with others, and working through the preceding exercises and questions, *what do you need to do now?* Use the space below to outline a plan of attack to move into the blessed future God has for you with confidence and hope.

_____

_____

_____

_____

_____

_____

9

IS IT A WALL OR A BOUNDARY?

Before you begin, watch the "Is It a Wall or a Boundary?" online video presentation from Stephen Arterburn at worthypublishing .com/books/Walking-Into-Walls/.

The Main Point

As we step into the future God has for us, the differences between building a wall and setting a boundary may not always be clear. And yet we need to understand the differences so that we can avoid a "more of the same" life and realize a "better than imagined" life ahead. Properly set boundaries will allow you to walk in freedom and light. You have a lot to look forward to!

Taking Stock

Have you been setting up walls that keep *you* restrained? Or boundaries that encourage a bright future? Mark which statements below represent a wall, and which ones represent a boundary. Then circle any statements that resemble ones you've made in the past six months.

- **We are done. You've run out of second chances.**
  Boundary/Wall

- **When you're ready to change, then maybe we can talk about moving forward with our relationship. But not until you deal with your issues!**
  Boundary/Wall

- **I will not be spoken to like that. I will discontinue the conversation until we both can get our emotions in check.**
  Boundary/Wall

- **The opposite sex can't be trusted, so I'm not going to take any risks.**
  Boundary/Wall

- **If you choose to act that way when I've told you that it hurts me, here is how I will respond . . .**
  Boundary/Wall

- **From now on, I am going to get the help I need, whether you want to be part of that or not.**
  Boundary/Wall

As you consider the answers you've just given, what might you need to do now in order to eliminate any remaining walls and start setting wise boundaries?

_____

_____

_____

Move Forward: For Personal Reflection

1. In what areas of your life do you need to replace walls with healthy boundaries?

    _____

    _____

2. How are you perpetuating the past? Where have you failed to draw a line in the sand to keep the past from being repeated?

    _____

    _____

3. Which lifelong patterns have you realized are no longer working?

    _____

    _____

4. Choose one of those lifelong patterns, and start brainstorming some new solutions here.

    _____

    _____

5. What are some of the truths you've realized while reading this book that you can use to start building healthy boundaries?

_____

_____

Move Forward: For Discussion

1. What are some of the emotions that boundaries should never be built on? Why are these emotions detrimental to healthy boundary-setting?

2. How can a person discern the false safety of a wall versus the authentic safety of a boundary?

3. Discuss the meaning of this statement: "A wall is a barrier, whereas a boundary is a beginning."

4. What role can we play in helping each other set good boundaries?

Listen for God's Voice

King Saul is a prime example in Scripture of someone who failed to set boundaries for himself, much less abide by the boundaries that were set for him. And he kept running into walls until it cost him the kingdom of Israel.

Read 1 Samuel 15:1-3, 7-26.

1. What clues are we given in v. 17 about one of Saul's walls from the past?

2. What does v. 24 indicate was another of Saul's walls?

3. List some of the boundaries that God himself set through the prophet Samuel?

4. How would Saul have been blessed had he heeded these boundaries?

5. What's your attitude toward boundaries? Do you typically resist them? Distrust them? Embrace them?

6. How can you avoid making Saul's mistakes?

Proverbs is packed with truths that speak to the benefits of exercising boundaries and the consequences of failing to work around our walls. Check out these samplings of God's wisdom.

Read Proverbs 17:9, 10, 13, 14, 19, 27-28; 18:7, 9, 13.

1. List some of the areas in our lives that Proverbs identifies as needing boundaries.

2. Which of these areas do you struggle with? Which ones are contributing to your success in life?

3. What are some of the stated consequences of failing to set and heed boundaries? What are some of the blessings?

What You Can Do Now

After reading chapter 9, pondering its message on your own, discussing its ideas with others, and working through the preceding exercises and questions, *what do you need to do now?* Use the space below to outline a plan of attack to replace your prison walls once and for all with helpful boundaries that will keep you on the path toward the blessed future God has for you.

_____

_____

_____

_____

_____

_____

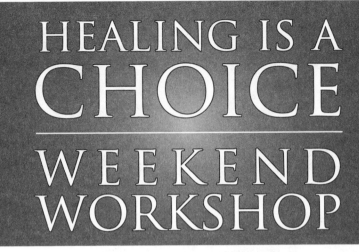

Transforming Lives
Through God's Truth

New Life Ministries is a non profit organization, founded by author and speaker, Stephen Arterburn. Our mission is to identify and compassionately respond to the needs of those seeking healing and restoration through God's truth.

New Life's ministry of healing and transformation includes:

- *A daily call-in radio and TV program, New Life Live!*
- *A nationwide counseling network*
- *Life changing weekend workshops*
  Healing Is a Choice Weekend
  Every Man's Battle
  Lose It for Life Weekend
- *Group Coaching*
- *Treatment for Drug and Alcohol addiction*
- *Books, CDs, Podcasts and others resources*
- *National Call Center manned 365 days a year*

**For more information
call 1-800-NEW-LIFE (639-5433) or
visit newlife.com**

WORTHY
P U B L I S H I N G

IF YOU LIKED THIS BOOK . . .

- Tell your friends by going to: http://worthypublishing .com/books/Walking-Into-Walls/ and clicking "LIKE"

  - Share the video promo by posting it on your Facebook page

  - Head over to our Facebook page, click "LIKE" and post a comment regarding what you enjoyed about the book

  - Tweet "I recommend reading #WalkingIntoWalls by @SteveArterburn"

- Hashtag: #WalkingintoWalls

- Subscribe to our newsletter by going to http://worthypublishing.com/about/subscribe.php

WORTHY PUBLISHING
FACEBOOK PAGE

WORTHY PUBLISHING
WEBSITE

Stephen Arterburn is a best-selling and award-winning author with over eight million books in print. His popular titles include *Every Man's Battle* and *Healing Is a Choice*. He has also been the editor of ten Bible projects, including the *Life Recovery Bible*. Arterburn founded New Life Treatment Centers in 1988 and is currently host of the radio and television show *New Life Live*. In 1996 he started the most successful traveling conference, Women of Faith, which has been attended by more than four million people. He and his wife live with their five kids in Fishers, Indiana.